The

Just wait with a loving longing, with a welcome in the heart for that great moment, the greatest moment in anybody's life—enlightenment. It comes...it certainly comes. It has never delayed for a single moment. Once you are in the right tuning, it suddenly explodes in you, transforms you. The old man is dead and the new man has arrived. — Osho

Bhagwan Shree Rajneesh
is now known simply
as Osho.

Osho has explained that
His name is derived
from William James' word
'oceanic' which means
dissolving into the ocean.
Oceanic describes the
experience, He says,
but what about
the experiencer? For that
we use the word 'Osho'.
Later he came to find out
that 'Osho' has also been used
historically in the Far East
meaning
"The Blessed One, on whom
the Sky Showers Flowers."

Published by
Sterling Publishers Private Limited

THE GIFT OF ENLIGHTENMENT

OSHO

A Sterling Paperback

STERLING PAPERBACKS
An imprint of
Sterling Publishers (P) Ltd.
L-10, Green Park Extension, New Delhi-110016
Ph.: 6191784, 6191785, 6191023 Fax: 91-11-6190028
E-mail: ghai@nde.vsnl.net.in
Website: www.sterlingpublishers.com

The Gift of Enlightenment
©2001, Osho International Foundation
ISBN 81 207 2339 2

Originally published in English as The New Dawn, Chapters 12-22
Copyright (c) 1989 Osho International Foundation.

Editing: Ma Shivam Suvarna, Ma Anand Anupam
Coordination: Swami Amano Manish

Published by Sterling Publishers Pvt. Ltd., New Delhi-110016.
Lasertypeset by Vikas Compographics, New Delhi.
Printed at Prolific Incorporated, New Delhi-110020.
Cover design by Sterling Studio

CONTENTS

INTRODUCTION

This book is full of the real stories and true-life dilemmas of those who are working towards more consciousness, struggling for an authentic life—and the patient, sparklingly clear responses from one who is awakened. The questions cover an immense range of experiences, from one woman's "loopy energy" to the "language of enlightenment," from questions about the role of journalism to the intricacies of relationship. And Osho has said that when He answers one person, He answers everybody; if it is not your question today, it may be tomorrow.

Osho speaks about the New Dawn: a complete break from the past which has led us to our present situation—a world perched on the edge of ecological and nuclear disaster, a population of unhappy, frustrated people—and the beginnings of a New Man who is loving, alive, nonserious, respectful of this earth; who possesses all those qualities that everyone, consciously or unconsciously, desires.

Does the world not look very dark right now? Every newspaper and magazine article on the world situation is pleading for changes in the way the world is managed, and in all of them there is a sense of despair. Scientists can say what needs to be done to reverse the slide towards ecological disaster, but they cannot force the politicians to carry out their suggestions. The despair and darkness are heavier than ever.

However, Osho reminds us of the well-known fact that the darkest part of the night is just before the dawn. He says, "A great adventurous moment is coming close to us; there is nothing to be feared. You cannot do anything to prevent it, but you can be in such a way that your very being prevents it."

In fact, the first few rays of the dawn are in sight, just creeping over the horizon. But don't search for them outside. The sun is waiting to rise in all of our inner worlds, we just have to look there. We are fortunate, in this age of darkness, where we have all lost the way to the inner, to have a man like Osho to remind us.

Around this illuminated being of Osho, small flames are tentatively flickering. In these pages you may catch the flame, you may get a glimpse of your own New Dawn.

Ma Shivam Suvarna

1

IF YOU WANT CONSOLATION, GO SOMEWHERE ELSE

I want to help you to see clearly how you are creating your own world. To me, you are your own world, and you are your world's creator. Neither your past life nor any God is deciding what is happening in your life; you are the decisive factor. Take responsibility for it. Be strong, have some stamina, and make an effort to change.

Beloved Osho,

From Your answer to the woman who falls in love with bank balances, not the man, I realized that I can't even see the man, let alone love him. I have accepted my mother's angry conditioning towards men. When a man comes to me with his love, I run away, which encourages him to chase me. This game I play is so ugly. Please Osho, help me to drop this garbage, to be able to see men and to know their beauty, their gifts, their love.

Dhyan Nidhi, before I answer your question I would like everyone to know that if you are not capable of understanding me when it is a question of your personal relationships then don't bring those questions to me, because I cannot lie and console you. I am not a consoler. Don't force me to be a baby-sitter.

When you bring a question to me, you have to be ready to understand my vision, my clarity, my understanding, even if it goes against your ego. It is bound to, because all your questions are arising out of the ego. That is your basic problem; all other problems are only by-products.

As far as I am concerned, I am not interested in your personal relationships; that is absolutely your own nightmare. You have chosen to suffer—suffer. But when you bring a question to me, then remember that I am simply going to say the truth of someone who can observe without being a party to anybody. This is not ordinarily the case in the world. Whenever you go to someone with a question about your personal relationship and the suffering it is bringing, the worldly way is to console you.

In some way, all the religions have been doing that for centuries. They have all found explanations so that nothing has to be changed; you are not to grow in consciousness and awareness. They only go on giving you homeopathic sugar pills—consoling you that it is your past life and its evil acts that are affecting your life, shadowing your life, bringing misery to you. All you can do is accept it and be patient, because God is compassionate and you will be finally forgiven. This is an opium; it keeps you half asleep.

People have chosen all these consolations because they help them to avoid taking the trouble of changing their consciousness, their understanding, their attitudes. Nothing has to be changed; you cannot do anything. So relax in your position, accept it as your fate, because if nothing can be done about it, the only thing possible is acceptance.

Acceptance brings a kind of peace—dead, hiding your despair, your anguish, your suffering. But knowing that nothing is in your hands; everything is in the hands of God...you are only a puppet. When he pulls your strings, you dance; whatever he wants to do with you, he does. It helps you to remain in a condition of being half asleep. And it also takes away the responsibility from you. You cannot do anything; hence you are not responsible for what is happening—you are not contributing to the suffering of yourself and the person you are related to.

And you can go on repeating the same vicious circle your whole life. Slowly, slowly you become accustomed, you become immune. You know this is how life is. That's why there has not been any revolution in human relationships.

Although men and women have suffered together, creating all kinds of troubles for each other, there has not been in ten thousand years any revolution, any change in their relationships. What your parents have been doing, you are repeating. Your children will learn from you, and they will repeat it. You know that this is how life goes on...you remember your parents, or perhaps even your grandparents. And your children are learning everything from you, and they know this is the way life has to be lived.

So if you want consolation, go somewhere else—any priest will be helpful: Catholic, Protestant, Hindu, Mohammedan, Jewish.

I am not here for consolation.

Consolation to me is poison.

I want to help you to see clearly how you are creating your own world. To me, you are your own world, and you are your world's creator. Neither your past life nor any God is deciding what is happening in your life; you are the decisive factor. Take responsibility for it. Be strong, have some stamina, and make an effort to change.

But first you ask the question, and if I don't answer then you feel rejected. Just the other day there was one question, "I have asked my question many times, and you are not replying. I feel very much rejected." You don't leave me any space. And if I answer it, then you feel hurt. My answer is going to hurt you— hurt you terribly, because my answer is going to open your wounds which you have been hiding, of which you may not be aware.

Just last night I was talking about Dhyan Om and his ex-girlfriend Latifa, because they were continuously fighting. It seems their whole psychology was completely fixed: each was trying to dominate the other, and both were strong people. Nobody was submissive and there was no solution.

If one was weaker and had submitted, seeing all the trouble, the problem would have remained but there would have been a cold war; undercurrents would have continued. But because both were strong personalities...and nothing is wrong in being strong, but they were misusing their strength. Every good thing can be misused.

It is not only weakness that creates problems, it is also strength that creates problems. If one of them were weaker, that person would have accepted the slavery and they would have been a good couple. Such good couples you can find everywhere. Their goodness consists only in the fact that the woman has surrendered. She has accepted for centuries to be secondary, not to try to dominate directly. But indirectly she goes on torturing, nagging, being bitchy; that is a natural outcome of an unwilling state.

Nobody can love slavery. Everybody hates it. And the man who has forced the slavery, rather than being your lover, becomes your enemy. So on the surface, just a thin layer of love...and underneath there is so much hate. But you are not aware of that hate because it is in the deep darkness of your unconscious.

People have been asking me how to avoid their wife's or their girlfriend's nagging, because it has become a continuous headache. In the name of love, what they are getting is not love but just a constant torture, very subtle. She may not say anything, she may simply bang the door, but she has said everything by banging the door, by dropping the plate, by beating the child. She may not say anything to the husband. But the child has not done anything and he has a good beating. And the husband knows that he is being beaten, not the child. To avoid this whole thing, he tries to escape from the home, to the office.

You know about the offices. The boss approaches first. Even before the janitor has reached the office to unlock it, to clean it, the boss is already there, sitting in the car. Then the janitor arrives, then the clerks start coming, then the manager comes.... And they all look happier in the office, where there is so much work, and they hope that by the weekend they will be able to relax for two days.

But those two days of the weekend prove to be the most terrible because they have to be at home for twenty-four hours. Clouds of misery surround them. For five days, the working days, they hope for the weekend, and at the weekend they pray to God,

"Finish this weekend as quickly as possible; the office is far better!"

I have heard, two men used to sit in the pub very late every day till the owner was about to close. He almost had to push them out, saying, "Now go home, it is illegal to keep the pub open any longer. It is the middle of the night. Get out!" Then reluctantly they would go.

One day, one man asked the other, "I know why I am sitting here, but what is the reason that you go on sitting here every day?"

The other one said, "My reason is my wife. As long as I can remain out of the home I have some dignity, some self-respect. The moment I enter the home, I have to enter with my tail between my legs. And immediately all my dignity, all my self-respect is destroyed. But why do you go on sitting here? I know perfectly well you are unmarried."

The first man said, "I go on sitting here just because I am unmarried—there is nobody waiting for me at home. I am hoping to get married."

He said, "This is strange, I am sitting here because I am married; you are sitting here because you are unmarried, there is nobody at home waiting for you. For me there is somebody waiting..."

What kind of relationships have we created?

Dhyan Om was very angry. You ask the question, and then your reaction is anger. That means you missed the point. Latifa was a little better. She was crying, and then laughing...and then crying, and then laughing. Whenever she understood the point she laughed, and whenever she became herself she cried. So this went on for a long time.

Shunyo is innocent—in a way very gullible. She thought this poor Om was presenting the sari to her because she understands him and his misery. This is something to be understood. I have been working with thousands of people for almost three decades.... Women never sympathize with women because they know from their own experience how bitchy they are! So they project the same bitchiness on every other woman; they never sympathize with the woman. They will always sympathize with the man: "Poor fellow, he is suffering so much in the hands of that monster."

This is one of the reasons why women are not yet liberated, because they cannot become a force together. They sympathize with the man; their sympathy is not for other women. With other women they have a relationship only of jealousy—if she has better clothes, if she has better ornaments, if she has a good car, if she has a better house. Their only relationship with other women is of jealousy.

But if every woman is jealous of every other woman, then naturally this is one of the fundamental causes of their slavery. They cannot become a force; otherwise they are half the number of people—they could have managed to become liberated long ago. Any time they wanted to be liberated there was nothing to prevent them. They are their own enemies.

Shunyo is innocent. She unnecessarily got into trouble by accepting the sari. She should have told Om, "This day when you are separating, it seems so outlandish; it proves you really are a crackpot. In one room you are deciding to separate and suddenly, in the middle of this separation business, you remember to present a sari to me."

Now he is saying that he had not purchased the sari from here. A few days before, Latifa had sent Om to Bangalore for some work and there he purchased the sari, with Latifa's money. And he wanted to give it to Shunyo because she understands him better than anybody else; she sympathizes with him, consoles him more than anybody else.

But I wonder why he was keeping that sari for so many days? If it was purchased in Bangalore with Latifa's money, when he had come back from Bangalore he should have given it to Shunyo. Why had he been keeping it only for the day when he would be separating? This shows a cunningness, a calculativeness. It was not purchased for Shunyo. It was purchased because it was certain that sooner or later he and Latifa will have to separate, because they are creating a constant scene in Lao Tzu House. So he brought the sari in case they have to separate and he will have to find another woman immediately.

It is just a coincidence that he found Shunyo. If it was purchased for Shunyo, he would have given it to her a few weeks before; that would have been natural, that he had gone and purchased it, and he had given it as a gift. But just yesterday, when he had to change his room and take his things—before doing that, just in the middle of all that turmoil—he remembered to give Shunyo the sari.

Shunyo has to understand it. This innocence can be misused by others.

Just a few days before, one woman, Patipada, was here. She wanted to be here but she was part of a small group that destroyed the commune in America, because they committed so many crimes that their crimes became a support to the American government.

This Patipada had even tried poisoning people, under the instructions of Sheela. And before things had come to a point where I was going to request the government to enquire into all the activities this small gang had done against the whole innocent commune, Sheela escaped. Patipada also escaped, and the day she escaped she came to see me just as I was going for a press interview. She was standing there in front of the door, and she said, "I am very grateful to you, Osho, but now perhaps I will never see you again. I am leaving this place tonight."

"But," I said, "why are you leaving, and why will you not be able to see me again?"

She said, "The situation is such."

It was only discovered later, when all the crimes were discovered, that she was also a partner in those crimes. That was the reason for leaving the commune, and that was the reason...because then in what way will she be able to face me? But she came here, and she knows perfectly well that I will forgive her; there is no problem about it.

It is human to err, and it is more human to forgive. I will not say it is divine to forgive. That is making forgiveness a superiority.

But she gave two hundred rupees to Shunyo, two hundred rupees to Nirvano, and two hundred rupees to Amrito just as a present.

Amrito and Nirvano both thought that this was a bribe so that she can be accepted into the commune, and they wanted to give that money back—it looked dirty. But Shunyo is innocent; she behaved the same with Patipada, thinking, "How sweet she is." She could not see the point, why in the first place she would give that money to her. It is because these three people look after me; to approach me, these three people are the key. And if they are satisfied with her then perhaps they will help her to get re-established in the commune.

But Shunyo was also hurt yesterday, because she was thinking it was because of Om's great understanding of her sympathy that he had given her the present.

One thing every woman has to remember is that man has divided you in such a cunning way that you can never become a force. You are jealous of each other; you don't have any sympathy for each other. You would rather sympathize with men—not your man of course! It has to be somebody else's man.

Shunyo has to grow in more understanding and more awareness. The only man who laughed at the whole matter and enjoyed it was Shunyo's boyfriend, Milarepa. He really enjoyed the whole thing. He proved to be a more understanding person. He did not jump into the tournament that was going on; he remained outside playing his guitar, thinking, "Let these fools decide whatever they want to do."

And people freak out so easily if anything is said which goes against their opinions and their habits. They don't even think about it, that I don't have any vested interest in their relationships—whether they are together or separate. Just because they ask the question, I feel it as part of my compassion to make things absolutely clear.

And once things are clear to you...they cannot be clear in anger, they cannot be clear when you are freaking out. They can be clear only when you meditate upon them. Whatever I say to you has to be meditated upon. You are not to be defensive about it, because there is no question—I am not attacking you. You all belong to me in the same way.

I would like you to be more individual, more free, more alert, more conscious, more meditative. And these situations can be great opportunities for meditation. But if you get angry, freak out, start defending yourself, then please don't ask such questions. I have no interest at all. Your relationship is your business.

My simple concern here is meditation. And this is very strange—rarely do you ask questions about meditation. That does not seem to be your main concern. To me, it is my ultimate concern, the only concern, and to you it seems not a priority—it is not the first item on your mind. Perhaps it may be the last thing on your laundry list, but certainly it is not the first; the first things are stupid things, trivia. You waste your time, you waste my time.

And I am ready even to help you to solve those problems just so that you can get rid of all this nonsense and have simple, loving relationships. But that will be possible only when meditation becomes your priority. Out of meditation, everything else will become graceful; you will be able to see deeply into your own acts, into your own behavior, and you will be able to have some compassion for the other person—his human frailty, the possibility of his committing mistakes.

When somebody commits a mistake you don't have to be angry, you have to be more compassionate, so that he does not start feeling guilty. Because you don't understand the psychology of things: if one person commits a mistake and you become angry—and your anger is justified because the mistake has been done by the other person—your anger creates humiliation in the other person. That humiliation becomes a wound which wants revenge. So the other person will wait until you commit a mistake—and you are not beyond committing mistakes—and then he will take revenge with a vengeance.

Never make anyone feel guilty, because if you make the person guilty he or she can only hate you; love becomes impossible.

That's why I repeat again and again:

Love needs as a basic foundation, meditation.

Only in the heart of meditation roses of love can grow. That is the right soil; there is no other way.

Dhyan Nidhi, your question is, "From your answer to the woman who falls in love with bank balances, not the man, I realized that I can't even see the man, let alone love him. I have accepted my mother's angry conditioning towards men. When a man comes to me with his love, I run away, which encourages him to chase me. This game I play is so ugly. Please Osho, help me to drop this garbage, to be able to see men and to know their beauty, their gifts, their love."

Now, if you really want to drop this garbage...your mother is in that garbage, and that will hurt you. You have been poisoned by your mother. Out of a hundred problems and troubles, almost ninety percent of them are because of your mothers because the child grows in the mother's womb. Even while he is in the womb, the mother's moods and emotions affect him. If the mother remains constantly angry, sad, gloomy, frustrated—if she does not want the child and the husband has forced her to have a child, if she is having the child unwillingly...all these things are going to affect the basic fabric of the child's mind. He is in the making. It is not only the flesh of the mother and the blood of the mother that the child will get; he will also get her psychology—not only her physiology.

So while a mother is pregnant she has to be very careful because a new life is being created inside her. Anything she is going to do—fighting with the husband, fighting with the neighbors, or being frustrated for any reason—is destroying and poisoning the child's mind from the very roots. Before he is born, he is already prejudiced.

It is not only your mother who is angry with men. Almost ninety-nine percent of women are angry with their husbands. The same is true about husbands: they are angry with their wives. But their anger does not affect the child so much, because the child is inside the mother's womb and the child starts growing under the shadow of the mother, not under the shadow of the father. The father remains only a casual visitor. In the morning he may give the child a kiss, pat him and go to the office. In the evening he may come and have a little talk with the child; otherwise, for twenty-four hours the child is learning everything from the mother.

That's why every language is called the mother language, because the father has no chance to speak to the child when the mother is present! Mother speaks, father listens—the child learns the language from the mother. And it is not only the language, all her attitudes....

Every woman is angry for the simple reason that she is not free, she is enslaved. And certainly the enslaver is the husband; he has become her prison.

You will be surprised to know that in all old scriptures of religions—they are all written by men—they are condemnatory of women, utterly condemnatory. One of the most famous saints of the Hindus is Tulsidas, who is read the most all over the country. Even in the villages, the uneducated listen to Tulsidas. His attitude towards women is so ugly—but he conditions the mind of man, all over the country.

He says that once in a while you have to beat the woman if you want to keep her in control. He categorizes woman with strange fellows: dhol, which means drum—unless you beat the drum it is useless; that's why the woman is categorized with the *dhol*. *Dhol*; *ganwar*, idiots; and *sudras*, the untouchables, the people who cannot even live inside the city. They are so dirty, according to Hinduism, that they have to live outside the town. For centuries they have been exploited, and they are doing the worst work, the hardest work. And they are the poorest; they don't have the dignity of human beings. "*Dhol, ganwar, sudra, pashu*"—and the animals. "*Dhol, ganwar, sudra, pashu, nari*"—and the woman. "*Ye sab tarn ke adikari*"—all these are in absolute necessity of being tortured.

And this man Tulsidas is one of the most prominent saints of the Hindus! To me, just this small statement is enough to declare that this man is neither a saint nor even a human being. But he has been conditioning the mind of man for three hundred years in this land. And he is not alone, he is simply repeating the old heritage of other scriptures.

The most intriguing and the most surprising thing is that women are his greatest audience. They listen to Tulsidas, they listen to such statements, and they don't revolt; they don't burn every book of Tulsidas, which they could do very easily. Tulsidas' books should be burned in every house—and every woman is capable at least of burning the books. His name should be erased from all over the country. But no, they worship his book as a holy book, and whatever he says as true.

I have been issued summons by courts because I have condemned Tulsidas on this point—that I have hurt the feelings of the Hindus. It is such a strange world: this man is saying such ugly things and no women's feelings are hurt. And when I say something against this statement, immediately the court issues a summons against me, an arrest warrant: I have hurt the feelings of religious people. Strange, what kind of religious people are these? They should be hurt by Tulsidas, not by me!

But Tulsidas is a man, and he is nourishing the egos of other men. And woman has been so unconscious that she is following man and his ugly ideas against the woman herself. At least no woman should read or allow the book in her house. And women should drag the publishers of those books to the court and say, "This book should be banned. It cannot be published because it is against half of the population of the country; a book that hurts half of the population of the country is not worthy of being in circulation."

But life as we have lived it up to now is mostly managed by man. It is a man-made society; it has no place for women. And the strangest fact is that women are not in sympathy with other women. Their minds are also conditioned in such a way that they are sympathetic to the man.

Once in a while this also happens—it is natural, but mostly it becomes suppressed by the time she gets married—that deep down a woman carries her mother's feelings; she has been against men. And I don't see why she should not be, there is every reason. Man has crippled the woman, has prevented her from education, has prevented her from financial independence, has prevented her movement in the society. She is encaged in the home. Her whole dignity, her whole joy as a social being is completely destroyed. Naturally, there is anger.

Dhyan Nidhi, you have accepted your mother's angry conditioning towards men. It is absolutely well-founded, but it is not going to help human society or create a better future. Past is past.

You should start looking at men with fresh eyes—and particularly in this place, where our whole effort is unconditioning, dehypnotizing. All the rubbish that you are carrying has to be thrown away; you have to become unburdened and light so that you can gain your own understanding, your own insight.

And the women here are not uneducated. They are financially capable of being independent; they are as intelligent as any man. There is no need for them to be angry against men. If your mother was angry...

perhaps she was not educated, perhaps she was not financially able to be independent. She wanted to fly in the open sky, but she was encaged—you are not.

This is one of the reasons why I cannot communicate to the vast majority of this country—because the man will not be willing to listen to me; it goes against his domination, his power. And the woman cannot understand me; she is not educated. Even if she can understand me, she is not financially able to be independent; she cannot revolt against the man-made society. In India there is nothing like a women's liberation movement—not even the talk of it. No woman ever thinks that there is any possibility of liberation. She has lost all hope.

But your situation is different. You are coming from countries where you have received education, and education makes you financially able to be independent. You need not be a housewife; it is not necessary for you to be married. You can live with someone you love without any marriage.

The woman has to fight for it—the woman has to make marriage an absolutely personal affair in which the government, the state, the society, nobody has any business to interfere.

You are in a totally different space than your mother. Now, carrying her anger and her conditioning is simply stupid. Just forgive her and forget her, because if you go on having this conditioning of anger against men, you will never feel complete—you cannot love men. And a woman or a man who is incapable of loving remains incomplete, frustrated.

And this way it creates a vicious circle. Your anger prevents you from love, because love means dropping anger against men and moving to the diametrically opposite polarity—instead of anger, love; instead of hate, love. A quantum leap needs courage. The vicious circle is that because of your angry conditioning you cannot love men, and because you cannot love men you become more and more frustrated, and your frustration makes you more angry—this is the vicious circle. Anger brings frustration; frustration makes you more angry, more violent, more against men. That brings more anger, and the circle goes on becoming deeper and deeper. And to get out of it becomes almost impossible.

You have to begin from the very beginning. The first thing is, try to understand that your mother lived in a different situation. Perhaps her anger was right. Your situation is different. Moreover, now that you are here with me, your whole situation is totally different. Here, carrying your mother within your mind is simply unreasonable. You have to live your life; you are not to live your mother's life. She suffered; now why do you want to make more suffering in the world? Why do you want to be a martyr?

Have every compassion towards your mother—I am not saying to get angry at your mother that she conditioned you. That will be again keeping you in anger, just changing the object from men to the mother. No, I want you to drop the anger completely. Your mother needs your compassion; she must have suffered. That created anger in her. But you are not suffering.

You put your anger aside and you have a fresh look at men. And particularly in my place...these men are not the same as you will find outside in the world. They have some understanding that man has done wrong, much wrong, to women. And they feel sorry for it.

But they have not done it. If their forefathers did it, it is beyond their power to undo it; what has happened, has happened. They have a deep apology in their hearts for what man has done to women. And you have to understand this, that these are a different category of people.

I am creating every possibility for the New Man—a man who is not contaminated by the past, who is discontinuous with the past. It is a difficult job; it is almost like hitting my head against the wall. But I am determined to go on hitting—I trust in my head! And the wall is very old and ancient. It may hurt me, but it has to fall; its days are finished. It has already lived more than its life span.

So have a fresh look towards men. Without man, a woman is incomplete, just as the man is incomplete without a woman. There is only one exception: if you become enlightened, then your inner woman and your inner man make a completion. But without enlightenment you remain half—you have to become complete by meeting with the other sex on the outside. Otherwise, everybody has both, because you are born out of the meeting of a man and woman; your father has contributed, your mother has contributed. You are carrying your father and mother both within you.

Sometimes it is only a question of a very small difference. For example, there are people known as 'the third sex'—what is their problem? Their problem is that their man inside is fifty percent and their woman inside is fifty percent; they equalize each other. Hence they are neither man nor woman. Mostly the difference is big enough—at least seventy-five percent woman, twenty-five percent man, or seventy-five percent man, twenty-five percent woman.

But sometimes the difference is very small: fifty-one percent woman, forty-nine percent man. Then it happens once in a while that the sex changes without your doing anything. The difference is so small that a little change in food, in atmosphere, a little change in your hormones—just by accident you were taking some medicine for something else—and it changes your chemical balance. And the difference was so small...

There have been many cases in the past in the courts around the world... A man marries a woman and after a few months the woman turns into a man. Now the problem is, what to do? Both are men. And they have to resort to going to the court. Physiologists came to figure out why such accidental sex changes happen, and now it is possible through scientific methods to change the sex. And many people are changing their sex.

Perhaps in the future it will become a fashion. I am certain about it—it will become a fashion. You will live up to thirty years as a man, and then you will go through a change and become a woman. If you can manage to live both sides of the coin in one life, why live only on one side? If you can know both banks of the river, know both banks. Your life will be richer, and at least you will not talk in the way old poets and philosophers have been talking for centuries, that "Woman is a mystery." Become a woman and know the mystery!

There is nothing, no mystery. Neither the woman is a mystery nor is the man a mystery; the mystery is when love happens between them. Alone they are dry deserts. When love comes as a spring it brings thousands of flowers to their being, and much juice, much greenness. Life is no longer just a drag, it becomes a dance.

Dhyan Nidhi, meditate more and be aware when your mother's voice starts speaking to your mind. Slowly, slowly put that voice to sleep. Don't listen to it; it will spoil your whole life. You have to learn how to love the man.

By loving, the man becomes more polite, nicer, a gentleman, loses his corners, becomes softer. Through love, the woman starts blossoming; otherwise she remains a closed bud. Only in love, when the sun of love rises, she opens her petals. Only in love her eyes start having a different depth, a different shine; her face starts having a joyous outlook. She has a deep transformation through love; she comes to maturity, of age.

So you get rid of the conditioning that your mother unconsciously has given to you. You have accepted it unconsciously. The way to get rid of it is to become conscious of it. It is a good beginning that you have asked. This is the beginning of consciousness—just the very ABC. You have to go far to change your mind completely, to be fresh, unconditioned, open and vulnerable.

And because of this conditioning you have been playing this ugly game, that whenever a man comes to you with his love, you run away—which naturally encourages him to chase you. That you enjoy, that he is chasing you. Every woman enjoys that. It is ugly; you are not aware of its deeper implications. It means you are the game; the man is the hunter and he is chasing the game. You are allowing a supremacy to man, unknowingly.

It has been traditionally given to you that the initiative in love should be taken by men, not by women; it is against a woman's grace. Those are all rotten ideas. Why be number two from the very beginning? If you love a man, why wait? I know many women who have waited for years because they wanted the man to take the initiative. But they have fallen in love with such men who were not going to take the initiative.

I know one woman in Bombay who was in love with J. Krishnamurti. Her whole life she remained unmarried, waiting for J. Krishnamurti to take the initiative. She is one of the most beautiful women—but J. Krishnamurti is not the type of man...he is utterly fulfilled within himself, he does not need anybody else to complete him. Obviously, he never took any initiative. And the woman, out of the conditioning of thousands of years, of course cannot take the initiative—that is against grace, that is primitive.

I know another woman in Ahmedabad who waited her whole life for Pandit Jawaharlal Nehru to marry her. Jawaharlal was not an enlightened man, and there was every possibility... And very strangely, in his old age he fell in love with Lady Mountbatten and they were writing such letters to each other that teenagers write. They were so foolish....

But this woman belongs to the richest family of Ahmedabad—I used to stay in their home—and she is so ugly.

Jawaharlal was a beautiful man; I cannot conceive that he would ever have thought of this woman when any woman would have been ready to marry him. But she was thinking only of her richness.

I know both the women. The woman who was in love with J. Krishnamurti used to come to see me also. I have seen in both these women's eyes such sadness...it would have been better if they had taken the initiative. There is no harm if the other person says, "Excuse me, I am not ready." He has that right, it is not an insult. It is simply his freedom to say yes or no.

I would like my women not to wait for the man to take the initiative. If they feel love for someone, they should take the initiative and they should not feel humiliated if the man is not willing. This will give them equality. These are small things which will make the liberation of woman possible.

But the woman has been always trying to be game. She attracts the man, she tries in every way to attract him by her beauty, by her clothes, by her perfume, by her hairdo, all that she can manage to do, her makeup...

She attracts the man, and once the man is attracted then she starts running away.

But she does not run too fast, either. She goes on looking back, to see whether that fellow is coming or not. If he is left far behind, she waits. When he comes again close, she starts running. This is stupid; love should be a clean affair. You love someone, you express your love and tell the other person, "You are not obliged to say yes; your no will be perfectly respected. It is just my desire. You need not unwillingly say yes to me, because that yes is dangerous unless you also feel love for me. Only then can our life become a completion."

A woman and a man in love can move into meditation very easily. Meditation and love are such close phenomena that if you move into meditation, your love energies start overflowing. If you really fall in love with someone who loves you, your meditative energies start growing; they are very deeply joined experiences. Hence I am in favor of both.

Okay, Maneesha?

Yes, Osho.

2

YOU GO ON DRINKING POISON

A s you are is absolutely right, worthy, respectable, and
there is no need to change it and create a phony
personality just because others want it. You have tried to
make others happy too much, and the total result is that
everybody in the world is unhappy.

Beloved Osho,

In Your presence, I feel showered with Your unconditional love
and compassion. My hungry heart is opening, and I have
experienced a lot of joy and stillness here in Your buddhafield. But
my feelings of unworthiness still dominate my life, and I'm
clinging to them so tightly that I despair of ever letting go. It has
been a long and serious road so far.
Dear Osho, will You please help me?

Prem Neerja, nobody is born unworthy. Everybody is equal in
the eyes of existence. But remember, equality does not mean
similarity. Everybody is equally unique.

The idea of unworthiness that is torturing you is torturing
millions of human beings. It is the people around you who make
you feel unworthy, undeserving, useless, good-for-nothing; this is
a secret conspiracy against the individual by the crowd.

Perhaps you are not aware that the crowd is the enemy of the
individual. The crowd does not like individuals; it likes only
phony people imitating each other. Anybody who stands alone, in
his own right, declaring his own freedom, doing his own thing

without any fear of consequences, will be condemned by the crowd.

The crowd cannot afford such rebels, because their very presence is dangerous—it may become a wildfire. Many others who are suffering in slavery may start revolting, seeing that it is possible to live your life according to your own light, that it is possible to have your own style, your own religiousness, your own morality—you don't have to belong to any crowd, you don't have to become a spiritual slave. If this idea spreads, there will be millions of people who have not died completely—in whose beings there is still a spark of life—who may explode into rebellion against the masses.

The masses are easy to control; hence, those people who are in power hate individuals. And this has been the story throughout human history. From the very childhood, the society in different ways—the parents, the teachers, the priests, the neighbors—from all directions the society starts encroaching upon the freedom of the individual. All their effort is to distract you from your own being; they want you to be somebody else, they don't want you to be yourself.

That is the cause of your feeling of being unworthy. It is natural—you can never be somebody else; however perfect your pretension and your hypocrisy is, deep down you will feel you have betrayed yourself. Deep down you can never feel contentment, self-respect, a pride which is natural to every being, a dignity which existence showers upon you just by giving you life.

If you are allowed to be yourself, you will never feel unworthy, because that will be your natural growth. If you are a rosebush, roses will blossom in you, and if you are a marigold flower, then marigold flowers will come. Neither the marigold flower feels it is unworthy nor the roses feel that they are special, higher, or holier. Even the smallest grass blade feels as dignified as the biggest star in the universe.

In existence there is no inferiority complex anywhere, and as a corollary there is no superiority complex either. The marigold is happy being a marigold; even the idea is stupid: "Why am I not a rose?"

It will be a very poor existence where there are only roses and roses and roses, and no other flowers. Roses will lose all their beauty. The variety of millions of flowers makes existence rich beyond all our dreams.

But the society wants you to be just a sheep. You may have the qualities of being a deer, or being a tiger, or being a lion, or being an eagle—all the varieties are possible in different individuals—but the society likes only one brand: everybody has to be a sheep. Now, if you force a lion to be a sheep, he is going to feel unworthy. You are imposing something upon him which is not natural.

This feeling of unworthiness is because of an imposition of unnatural demands upon you, made by everybody around you. Nobody likes you as you are; everybody wants you to be this, to be that. Of course if you fulfill their demands you will be loved, respected, honored, but it is very dangerous and very costly; you will have to lose yourself. You will become just a hypocrite, and what will be the gain? What is their respect, what is their honor, what are their rewards? They cannot balance the loss—you have lost your soul. They can give you Nobel Prizes, but even a thousand Nobel Prizes cannot make up for the loss that you have suffered in the transaction. You have lost your very space in existence, your very territory, your most significant essential being and consciousness.

I can understand your problem, Prem Neerja, and I don't think you are incapable of understanding it intellectually. You do understand, but just intellectual understanding never brings any change; it brings you more trouble. It makes you aware that you have done something very stupid, and now you have become an expert in doing that stupidity. Now that is your expertise—for that expertise you are paid, honored, respected, so you cling to it.

This becomes a tremendous dilemma. It creates a state of schizophrenia. You know that what you are doing is wrong, but this knowing is only intellectual; it has not penetrated into the deeper parts of your being from where actions arise.

Intellect is an inactive force. It has not become your meditation, it is still your mind, and mind is absolutely impotent. So you understand intellectually that you are doing wrong, and the same intellect says that this is the only thing that you know— unworthy or worthy, but this is the only thing that gives you credit, makes you respected by the crowd. Don't leave it, because you don't know where you have lost your soul and whether you will be able to find it again. You don't even remember the way back home.

So you go on clinging to that which intellectually you know is not right. You are destroying yourself, but you go on drinking the poison, because you have forgotten the way to your home.

Just the other day, Latifa was crying, and today all the clouds have disappeared. She has taken the bold step. Intellectually she has been thinking and thinking for almost an eternity...because misery lengthens time so long—one hour passes as if it is one life. Hence I say she has been suffering as if for the whole eternity, knowing perfectly well—because I was continuously hammering her—that if you are miserable in a situation and the doors are open, why don't you get out of that situation?

She wants to get out, but clings; she is afraid of the open, is afraid of the fresh air, is afraid of the unknown. Her deeper being feels the pull, the challenge, the excitement of the unknown, but her superficial mind thinks of security, safety. And who knows?— you may fall into a worse condition. At least this misery is well known, and you have somehow become accustomed—in fact, so habituated that a fear somewhere in the corner of your being lurks: are you capable of surviving without it?

It is miserable but at least there is something. You are not alone, and you are not empty; you are full of misery, and you can depend on it that tomorrow also the misery will be there. You need not be worried that tomorrow maybe you will be empty and alone. So one becomes a mess inside.

But finally, Latifa came to her senses, took the bold step. And today she wrote a letter to me of tremendous gratitude, saying that she feels as if a cancer has been removed from her being; she feels clean, healthy, happy, light—the whole burden has disappeared. And this was the cancer she was clinging to.

But you can experience the joy and the freedom and the lightness and the open sky, only when you drop clinging; there is no other way.

But people are such that even when they have come here and they have been listening to me, they are managing what to listen to, what not to listen to. Whatever gives nourishment to their prejudices, they are open to, very happy that their convictions are being supported. The moment I say something that goes against their convictions—and those convictions are their misery, the foundation of their suffering and their hell—immediately they close themselves. But how long can you keep yourself closed? I go on hitting you from every dimension, every direction. Sooner or later you have to listen.

Then too, such is human stupidity that people start defending themselves. I sometimes wonder why you are wasting your time. If you are here to defend yourself, that you can do very well wherever you are. It will be easier to defend yourself somewhere else; here it will be very difficult. I will not allow you to defend yourself, because by defending yourself you are defending all your miseries; they are synonymous. You and your miseries, you and your suffering, you and your ideology—they are not separate.

Your personality is your hell, and I have to hammer it and bring out your individuality, which is a totally different phenomenon—that which you had brought with you when you were born. This personality is a cover that has been put over you by the society; it is a mask. But you have lived with the mask so long that you have started thinking it is your original face. In their sleepiness people go on defending that which is their cancer.

One woman today wrote to me that she hates Hymie Goldberg. I could not believe that somebody can hate a poor fellow like Hymie Goldberg! But perhaps she has an anti-Jewish mind...just the name of Hymie Goldberg and her Nazi upbringing feels hurt that I am making Hymie Goldberg almost a great hero. It is true, I am going to write a biography of Hymie Goldberg.

In the same question, the same woman says, "I don't like you to laugh with us." It seems she is also against laughter. I rarely laugh, but once in a while I want simply to join with you—so as not to give you the feeling that I am separate from you. I want to be one amongst you, not somewhere high up, very serious—a stone golden Buddha.

Certainly, Gautam Buddha did not laugh; neither is there any reference anywhere that Jesus ever laughed. These people are serious people.

I am not serious. I have been telling you again and again that I am absolutely nonserious, but you don't take it seriously! You think I must be joking...it is such a difficult problem, how to solve it?

And when I read this woman's question, I remembered Nadam's question yesterday...he was telling me that a few scientific researchers have found the G-point in the vagina of women. I could not figure it out, why it should be called "G-point."

I have also found a G-point. It is not in the vagina, it is in everybody's belly—just behind your navel. And it is meaningful to call it the G-point because it creates giggling. It is absolutely stupid to say there is a giggling vagina, but a giggling belly is a well-known fact. You know about belly laughter—a real laughter always comes from your belly.

So I don't care about your scientists; my own research says that the G-point is in everybody, man or woman, in the belly, behind the navel. And perhaps this woman's G-point is either paralyzed or is crippled, damaged—something is wrong with her G-point! Here she should expose herself; her G-point can start functioning. Amongst so many G's, how can you remain serious?

I have heard.... Two small kids, twins, started their first day at school and their teacher asked them, "What are your names?" They were looking so beautiful, so absolutely alive. Dressed in the same way, it was almost impossible to figure out who is who. So she asked, "What are your names?"

One said, "My name is Ronald Reagan, and my brother's name is Richard Nixon." The teacher could not believe it. She thought, "These kids are playing a joke on me, they are making fun of me." She immediately phoned their home and said to their mother, "Mrs. Johnson, your two kids have come and when I asked their names, one said his name is Ronald Reagan and that his brother's name is Richard Nixon. I could not believe it; that's why I am phoning. Are they making fun of me?"

She was in for a great surprise, because from the other end of the phone the woman shouted very angrily, "You have some nerve to call me Mrs. Johnson. I am Miss Johnson and they are my kids, and when you have two bastards, what names can you give them? If you were in my place, would you be able to suggest two other names for two bastards?"

Just watch life, and your G-point will start functioning!

Prem Neerja, you have fallen prey, a victim to what people have said to you. This commune is to erase all that has been said to you, and accept you the way you are. As you are is absolutely right, worthy, respectable, and there is no need to change it and create a phony personality just because others want it. You have tried to make others happy too much, and the total result is that everybody in the world is unhappy. Everybody has tried to make others happy, but do you see the total result? Everybody is unhappy.

I teach you to be happy, I don't teach you to make others happy. In your happiness, if there is some truth, some vitality, it will spread—it will help others also to be happy. But that should not be the criterion; that should not be the ideal of your life. You are making others happy, they are making you and others happy, and everybody is unhappy because everybody is pretending.

People can be happy only in one way—there are not two ways—if they are authentically themselves. Then the springs of happiness start flowing...they become more alive, they become a joy to see, a joy to be with; they are a song, they are a dance. But they are not dancing for anybody's approval, nor for anybody's appreciation; they are dancing out of their own abundance of happiness, out of their own joy.

This whole world can be a dancing world, full of songs and full of music, full of creativity and full of life and laughter. But the basic strategy that has been followed up to now has to be completely destroyed, without mercy.

The new minister stood at the church door, greeting parishioners as they departed after the end of the service. The people were generous in complimenting the clergyman on his sermon, except one fellow who said to him, "Pretty dull sermon, Reverend." And a minute later, the same man appeared again and said, "Pretty dull sermon, Reverend."

Once again the man appeared, this time muttering, "You really did not say anything at all, Reverend." When he got the opportunity, the Reverend pointed out the man to one of his deacons, "Ah," said the deacon, "don't let that guy bother you. He is a poor soul who goes around repeating whatever he hears other people saying!"

This is a very strange and insane world. Everybody is living in some way falsely, just to get appreciation, just to hear people's clapping. Everybody is so hungry for attention. The people you think of as great leaders are almost beggars as far as attention is concerned; that's all their whole life is devoted to—how many people are looking up to them. That gives nourishment to their ego. And they are ready to do any nonsense if they are promised, "More and more people will be attracted towards you; you will get more attention."

I have a strange story to tell you. It is not fiction, and it is about one of the most famous men, Abraham Lincoln. He had a very ugly face. He came from a very poor family; his father was a shoemaker. He himself was chopping wood just to get enough money to go to school—a very poor heritage.

His face was certainly not attractive; it was repulsive. And when he stood for the presidential election.... His intelligence was great; perhaps there has been no other man in America of such great intelligence. His rationality, his logic, his ways of arguing his case were superb. But his personality was poor, just because of his face.

The first day when he started his election campaign, a little girl... And as far as my understanding goes, that little girl should

have the whole credit for Abraham Lincoln's becoming the
president of America, although nobody bothers...nobody even
thinks about that little girl, or to find out who she was. She came
close and she said, "Uncle Lincoln, with this face you cannot win
the presidency. I have a small suggestion: if you grow a beard and
mustache, most of your face will be covered, and the beard and the
mustache can be given a shape that can change your whole
profile."

A little girl...but she was looking attentively at his face; she
was interested in his arguments. But women are more aware of
physical beauty even from their very childhood. She figured out
that if he grows a beard and a mustache, much of his face will be
covered. Then a new face can be created by giving shape to the
beard and to the mustache. And it appealed to Lincoln. He was
himself worried what to do with his face. He started growing his
beard...and now you don't see in his photographs or his statues
that his face was ugly. All that ugliness is covered by his beard and
mustache. In fact, that beard and mustache have given him a new
personality.

People have forgotten, but Lincoln did not forget. After
becoming the president, the first letter that he wrote was to that
small girl, thanking her, "Your suggestion worked." He was a man
of great humbleness and great understanding.

But this world does not look into the inner being. It does not
look at your intelligence, your talents, your creativity, your
potentiality. It simply looks at the outer, superficial personality.

And because you are continuously asking for attention, you
have to concede to the people; you have to compromise on every
step with them if you want to be accepted as worthy. And the
problem is that whatever you do, you cannot be absolutely false;
something of the real will remain, and that will be your
unworthiness.

It will hurt you that you have not been able to succeed in being
a complete success in the world.

Anybody who wants to be a success in the world, anybody
who is ambitious and egoistic, is going to suffer the same problem

as you are suffering, Prem Neerja. But the problem is very simple and can be dropped immediately, without any effort: just a simple understanding that you don't need anybody's attention; on the contrary, what you need is a deep contentment with yourself. And that is possible only if you are real.

What others say, don't be worried about; it does not matter. The only thing that matters is your inner happiness, your peace, your silence, and finally your realization of your eternal life.

You are asking, "What should I do with my unworthiness? It still dominates my life and I am clinging to it so tightly that I despair of ever letting go." Just a little understanding is needed— not much effort, because it is you who are clinging to it; it is not clinging to you.

There is a Sufi story that a river was in flood, and a few people were standing on the bank watching the river rising higher and higher. A Sufi mystic was also standing there. Sufis use just a blanket, a woolen blanket to cover their body; they don't use anything else. In fact, the name Sufi is derived from woolen blankets. In Persian, *suf* means wool, and *sufi* means one who uses only wool.

So with his blanket, he was also standing there watching other people, and then suddenly they saw a beautiful blanket, a woolen blanket floating down the river. A young man could not resist. Although everybody said it was dangerous—the river was in flood, and it was a huge river—the young man said, "That blanket I cannot lose." He jumped.

But it was not a blanket, it was a wolf, alive. So as he caught the blanket, the blanket caught him! He started shouting, "Save me!" Everybody asked him, "What do you mean by saving? Just drop that blanket!" He said, "It is not a blanket that I can drop. Now it is a question of whether the blanket drops me or not—it is a wolf!" It was just that they had seen the wolf's body, which looked like pure wool.

The Sufi wrote in his diary, "What I saw today was a real problem. Up to now I have seen people wondering how to drop this, how to drop that.... Those were all unreal because the problems were not clinging to them, they were clinging to their problems. It was not a question of any help; if they wanted to drop it, they could drop it."

The Sufi wrote in his diary, "But today it was totally different; it was a real problem. It was beyond that poor man's ability to drop it, because he was not clinging to it; now the wolf was clinging to him, and the wolf took him down to his grave."

It is good that wolves are not clinging to you. Whatever you are clinging to, all are just false ideas given by others to you. And the reason why you are clinging to them is that you are afraid that without them you will be almost naked, you will be empty, and you will be moving in an unknown space.

But I want to say to you that moving every moment into the unknown is the greatest blessing of life. Remaining with the known is sheer boredom, every day the same. Then what is the point of living? You have lived it many times, many days.

My encouragement to you is:

Love change, love the unknown.

Risk everything known for the unknown, and you will always be in an ecstatic state. You will always be a gainer, because the unknown has hidden treasures only for those who can drop the known. But I can only say it to you; the dropping has to be done by you. It has to be your decision, your commitment—only then will it bring joy.

Beloved Osho,

I have heard You say that we are all enlightened, and that we have just all forgotten it. Did we forget it at a precise time, and if so, why?

Prembodhi, yes we have forgotten it at a precise time, and I will tell you why.

Just try to remember backwards—how far back can you go? Four years of age, or at the most when you were three years of age. Beyond that comes an absolute blank—no memory, no remembrance.

One thing is certain, that in those three years many things must have happened. You must have cried, you must have been loved, you must have been left alone, you must have been afraid in the dark night—a thousand and one experiences must have happened. You may have fallen, you may have been hurt, you may have been seriously sick...but you cannot remember anything. It seems as if in those three years, nothing was recorded by your memory mechanism.

That's exactly the time when you forgot your self-nature. Let us say it in another way: the precise moment you forgot your enlightenment and the language of it, is the moment when you started remembering the world and thousands of other things of the world. When you started remembering others, you forgot yourself.

Now if you are fifty years old, for forty-seven years you have been remembering the whole world of things and people and events, so you have gathered a thick wall of memories. Behind this thick wall of memories—which goes on growing every day, thicker and thicker—is hidden that small time in the beginning of your life when you were utterly innocent. Even memory was not formed—you lived each moment and you died to that moment, and were born again.

In those three years, your life was moment to moment. You did not bother about the past, you did not bother about the future; you were so involved, so totally and so intensely in the moment, collecting seashells on the beach, or running after butterflies in the garden, or collecting wildflowers in the forest, as if that were all. There was no past, no future; you lived in the present in those three years. And those were the days of your glory, those were the days of your golden experience.

So I can say that it depends on everybody; it may be either four years or three years. For girls it will be three years, for boys it will be four years. Girls are one year ahead, they mature sooner. Sexually they mature one year sooner than the boys; mentally also they mature one year earlier than the boys. So girls can remember backwards to the age of three, and boys generally will be able to remember back to the age of four. That's where you have lost your treasure.

And you are asking why. It is because you became interested in the vast world around you. And you went on becoming more and more interested; you became so curious about everything, you wanted to know everything. Just listen to small children—they go on asking all kinds of questions, they are untiring. You get tired, but they are so excited—they have entered into a new world.

For nine months they were in the mother's womb, in utter darkness—no excitement, no problem, no responsibility, no companionship, just utter silence and relaxation. Then those three years, when their memory system was starting to be built up, their intellect was starting its ABC...by the age of three or four, they were able now, with a memory system and an intelligent, enquiring mind to go in search of this vast world—millions of things to know, unending pastures to be discovered. Naturally, in all this excitement, they forgot one thing: their own being. They went out and out and out, and farther and farther away from the home.

They reached to the stars, and now the home is so far away that they have even forgotten the way they had followed. And they don't know exactly what it was in those three years...just deep down in the unconscious some feeling has remained like a shadow—that it was beautiful, that it was very peaceful, that it was majestic, miraculous, mysterious, that everything was a wonder, that every moment brought new experiences and joys. Just faint echoes, far back...you cannot say if they are real or you are imagining them, or if you are remembering from your dreams. It has become almost a dream.

The why is very simple: because the world was very intriguing, very interesting to enter, to enquire.

It is natural. I am not saying that you should not have done this. You would not have been able to avoid it, and it would not have been good to avoid it. It is good that you have gone so far. Now that you have known the world and experienced everything good and bad, bitter and sweet, beautiful and ugly, have seen pleasures and have seen pain, you are again becoming interested to know what is your self-nature.

Your self-nature is enlightenment.

I was reading one story, which is significant in a totally different context—which was not supposed to be part of the story. I don't think that whoever invented the story had thought about it. The story is:

One day a black man showed up at the gates of heaven and was met by Saint Peter. "I would like to be admitted to heaven," he said.

"Fine," said Saint Peter, "but first tell me what you have done lately which would permit you to be admitted."

"Well," said the black man, "I marched in a civil rights march."

"A lot of people did that," said Saint Peter. "Maybe there is something else?"

"Yes," said the black man. "I got married at twelve o'clock noon."

"What is so unusual about that?" asked Saint Peter.

"I married a white woman," said the black man.

"When was that?" asked Saint Peter.

"Ah, about two minutes ago," said the black man.

As I was reading this, I remembered a scientific calculation. They say that if we think of existence just in terms of one day—as if the whole existence is twenty-four hours, reduced into this small measurement, so that at twelve in the night the existence began, the stars formed, the solar systems arose.... And they have the given exact hour when—for example, at four o'clock in the morning, at six o'clock in the morning—our solar system was born. Then our earth separated from the sun, just at eight o'clock in the morning; then the moon separated from the earth, just at eleven o'clock in the morning.

The earth for the first time saw life exactly at twelve o'clock noon, and man came into existence just two minutes later; that is, at two minutes after twelve o'clock.

If we measure the whole existence in terms of twenty-four hours, we have come into existence just two minutes ago.

Reading this story, that the black man said, "Ah, about two minutes ago," I remembered that calculation of the scientists. This poor negro married a woman at twelve o'clock, and then he must have been shot two minutes later when he was coming out of the church, because whites cannot allow a black man to marry a white woman. So only two minutes he remained married.

If we go into more details—that if two minutes ago, man came into existence—then just fifteen seconds ago, a Gautam Buddha was born. Then enlightenment and the whole idea of enlightenment is not more than fifteen seconds old.

And we have still twelve hours more, if Ronald Reagan allows. Ronald Reagan is just a representative of all the mad politicians of the world. If they allow, then we still have twelve hours to evolve. If in fifteen seconds Gautam Buddha, Pythagoras, Lao Tzu, Mahavira, Jesus, Ramakrishna, Raman Maharishi,

J. Krishnamurti, Gurdjieff—if all these people have happened just in fifteen seconds, then the coming twelve hours, if man remains on the earth...one cannot imagine how fruitful these coming days can be.

What a great potential is ahead of us! And we have been on the earth only for two minutes. These foolish politicians are trying to commit suicide at a moment when we should be evolving as fast, as quickly as possible, because half the time of existence is gone—only half the time remains.

In this remaining time, the whole humanity has to become enlightened. If we can avoid this coming war, then this will be the new dawn of a totally new consciousness, of a totally new and fresh life, with a fragrance it has not known before. It is in our hands.

Okay, Maneesha?

Yes, Osho.

3

WORDS FROM THE SILENCES
OF YOUR HEART

The positive person has to become assertive; he has to come into the light. Otherwise the world is left in the hands of the negative people, and these negative people are the cause of preventing others from seeking and searching.

Beloved Osho,

I have written many beautiful words about You and about Your books—words that seem to come from some place either beyond or deep inside when they happen. And afterwards I feel almost ashamed, as though I have said something which I have no right to say.

In these years of being with You, I know I have changed. Layers and layers have disappeared, and a silence has arisen which is never so far away that it feels out of reach. Yet I often wonder if the clarity I feel coming out of this silence is only "so-called"—some kind of arrogance in disguise, or some imagining, unknown to me. I don't know if this is a question, or three questions, or an apology. Beloved Osho, could You help me sort it out?

Deva Sarito, life is such a mystery that the more you know the more you become aware of your ignorance. Or in other words, the more you know it, the less you know it. And the day you know it all, you know nothing.

It has been said that science starts from not knowing and ends in knowing—that's exactly the meaning of the word 'science': knowing. And religion starts from knowing and reaches to its climax in not knowing—because not knowing is another name of innocence. And if religion cannot bring you back your childhood, and the freshness of childhood, and the wondering eyes of childhood, it is not religion at all.

Whatever is happening to you is perfectly the way it should happen. You have every right to say what you have experienced, what you have felt, what changes you have gone through. It is most important to say it, because it is unfortunately the situation that people who know nothing about me even write books against me.

All over the world, in all the languages, people who have never come in contact with me, have never heard me, feel perfectly right in writing all kinds of lies and rumors and allegations without any foundation, without any factuality behind them. The negative person is always very articulate, because to say no, you don't need any intelligence; any idiot can do it. But to say yes needs tremendous courage, and a great intelligence. And the people who say yes, the people who feel yes, are always keeping their secret hiding in their heart. This creates a very unbalanced situation. Those who don't know me go on writing anything, out of the blue.

Now there is an article in a German magazine, *Spiegel*, saying that I am trying to come to Germany and create a commune in Germany on the same lines as was created in America. So the government has to be aware, and the people of Germany have to be aware. Now, from where do these people get these ideas? I have not even dreamt about going to Germany. Even if they want me to be there, I will refuse. A few days ago in Israel, a Hebrew newspaper had an article saying that the people of Israel have to be clearly aware of the danger, because I am planning to come to Israel. And they say my strategy is that I will be converted to the religion of the Jews, and once I am a Jew, then I will declare that I am the incarnation of Moses!

What to do with these people?—and people read them, people believe them. And the people who know me, who have come into deep inner communion with me, who have experienced me, remain silent.

It is not new. It is part of a strange human psychology. The positive person is humble; even to say something he feels embarrassed, because he knows that whatever he is going to say is not going to be up to the experience that he had. It is going to fall very short; hence the embarrassment.

But the negative person has no fear, no embarrassment. He has not experienced anything. And to deny or to lie, or to create a fiction, is sensational. The people who have been writing against me...all the publishers are eager to publish their books—without knowing what they are writing, all kinds of rubbish. And a few of my sannyasins who have been with me from the very beginning have written books just to answer those lies and allegations, with facts and figures, with solid arguments.

The publishers are not willing to publish them. They say there is no sensation in it. Lies have sensation; the truth is non-sensational. And the masses are interested in sensationalism, they are not interested in knowing the truth. Truth is simple and plain.

But this situation has to be reversed; there is a limit to everything. The positive people have to come out in the light, and tell with emphasis their own experiences and what they understand about me and my relationship to my people. Unless they come out and do it, they are in an indirect way helping the negative people. Because if those negative people are not contradicted, it becomes an argument in their favor—why are they not contradicted?

So I can understand, Sarito, that you have experiences to express but it is always bound to be something not absolutely the experience. It is going to be something far below. But still it will help people to understand both sides. The negative is articulate, but is meaningless; it is not going to help anybody. It can only prevent people from coming to me. And the people who are writing all those negative books and articles—they cannot help anybody either. So they are really public enemies.

The positive person has to come out so the negative people can be contradicted, and so that those who are in search of truth, in search of silence and peace, can feel a possibility: if they come here, maybe if it is happening to other people, it can happen to them also. You will be opening doors, and you will be giving invitations to new sannyasins, to new seekers.

So don't keep it as a secret. Don't enjoy it inside yourself; share it with as many people as possible, with all the news media, so that you can reach to the farthest corners of the world.

And the positive person has many problems which the negative does not have. First, the positive person starts thinking, "Perhaps my silence, my joy, my bliss, is just imagination." The negative person has no problem; he knows exactly that it is imagination, there is no problem about it! The problem arises only to the positive person—because it is not imagination.

Living here for years... Imagination is a very momentary phenomenon; you cannot go on living in imagination for twelve years, fifteen years. It is possible to live in imagination for a few moments—imagination is not reality; imagination is just like soap bubbles. For a moment they can shine in the sun, create a rainbow, and then they are gone and all those rainbows disappear.

And one thing more you have to understand, for yourself: you cannot imagine silence; that is not in the nature of things. You can imagine all kinds of thoughts, but you cannot imagine thoughtlessness. Nobody has ever been able to do it, it is almost impossible. You cannot imagine blissfulness. You don't have any idea, how can you imagine it? Imagination needs some kind of experience; then you can project it. But blissfulness you don't know.

You can imagine misery perfectly well. You are so deeply rooted in misery that there is no problem. You know it, you can imagine it, you can exaggerate it, you can magnify it a thousandfold; it is in your hands. But blissfulness you don't know. Anything that you don't know is not possible for you to imagine.

So if you are feeling silence, peace, bliss; if you are feeling changes happening in you, in your consciousness, it is not imagination.

Secondly, you are worried that it may be "some kind of arrogance in disguise." One who is aware that his experiences may be some kind of arrogance, has really gone beyond arrogance, because arrogance never recognizes itself. The egoist never recognizes that he is egoistic; the arrogant cannot even think that he is arrogant.

To be worried that perhaps it may be arrogance is part of humbleness. Only a humble person becomes concerned that he should not say anything, he should not do anything that may bring arrogance from the back door. He knows the misery of arrogance, he knows the pain and the anguish of arrogance. He does not want to get into that trap again. But if you are aware, arrogance cannot come close to you, just as when you have light in your house, darkness cannot come in.

Gautam Buddha used to say, "You should be like a house which has light inside. When the house, its doors, its windows, are showing light, thieves don't come close. But when the house is dark and there is no light, it is an opportunity for thieves." And by thieves he means all that destroys your beauty, your grandeur, all that takes away your treasures. Arrogance, ego, aggressiveness, superiority, the idea of being special—all are destroying you and your peace; they are destroying your nobodiness.

You cannot imagine nobodiness. It is almost like...a beggar can dream of being a king—in fact beggars always dream, and in their dreams they fulfill the desires which they cannot fulfill in their actual waking lives. But nobody has ever heard of a king dreaming about himself being a beggar; that is unknown. Why should one dream of being a beggar? The hungry person can dream that he has been invited to a royal party; he can dream about delicious food—he has to, just to hide his hunger. But the man who is living in the palace and eating delicious food is not going to dream that he is hungry; that is just illogical, unpsychological.

We dream only of things which we don't have; we imagine things only which we don't have. But once you start having real experiences, those experiences start changing your lifestyle, your responses to situations; you can start feeling constantly within you a coolness, a grace, a gratitude towards existence, and out of this peacefulness, silence, beauty, all your actions arise...they also have something of it. Your words come out from the silences of your heart; they also have some music from their original source.

It is a well-known fact: a man like Jesus was uneducated, but no rabbi in the whole history of Judaism, four thousand years— and Jewish rabbis are great scholars, unparalleled in any other religion—but no Jewish rabbi has spoken the way an uneducated carpenter's son, Jesus, spoke. And he knew nothing of scripture, he knew nothing of the art of oratory. Even those who were not in agreement with him had to say, "One thing we cannot deny: nobody has ever spoken the way he speaks."

And he is using simple words, ordinary words used by common people, but on his lips those ordinary words have a changed quality. They are coming from a depth; they are bringing some fragrance with them, they are bringing some authority of his experience. The same words are available

...all the Christian missionaries are repeating the same words every day. But you don't feel any impact, you don't see... Why the difference?

The difference is that Jesus was speaking out of experience, and these people are speaking only out of their education. For Jesus, it was his life. For these missionaries, it is their salary; it is their livelihood, not their life. For Jesus, what he was saying was so important that he was ready to sacrifice his life, but not to compromise on any ground. But these missionaries, if somebody gives them a better salary, will change their religion immediately. These are professionals. Their words don't have any depth. Their words are not alive, but corpses. They look similar, they sound similar, but you can see when you hear a missionary....

One of the most famous missionaries in both parts of the world, East and West, was Stanley Jones. He used to live for six months in the East—he had a beautiful ashram in the Himalayas—and for six months he used to live in the West. I have come across many missionaries, but the caliber that Stanley Jones had, none of them have had. He was a genius. But even a genius cannot put life into words that are not his experience.

I told him...because he used to stay very near to where I was a teacher in the university, and slowly we became very intimate. He was a sincere man. I said, "There is a difference—you may accept it, you may not accept it. These are the same words spoken by Jesus, which you speak every day in your sermons, but something is missing. They sound the same; they are exactly the same words. And perhaps you are pronouncing them better than Jesus. He was uneducated, you are a genius"—and he was one of the best speakers—"and Jesus has nothing as far as the art of oratory is concerned. But his words had a life, his words had wings; they reached you as alive beings, not just corpses. Not just stuffed, dead birds, looking alive."

He was silent for a moment and he said, "Perhaps you are right. Whatever I am saying is my education, is my scholarship, is my lifelong learning. What Jesus was saying was not his learning; he never went to any school. What he was saying was his experience; his words were coming from a living source."

The positive person has to become assertive; he has to come into the light. Otherwise the world is left in the hands of the negative people, and these negative people are the cause of preventing others from seeking and searching.

I have always liked a story by Turgenev—a Russian novelist, one of the best the world has ever known. If you are going to choose ten great books, you will have to give one place to Turgenev without fail. Out of all the literature in all the languages in the world, he may claim more, but one is absolutely certain. He has written a small story, *The Fool.*

In a small village there was a very simple man. His simplicity was such that he almost looked like a simpleton, and the whole village condemned him as the idiot. Out of his simplicity he used to do things, and the cunning people all around condemned him. He became so much afraid even to say a single word, because whatever he would say, he would be immediately criticized, condemned. He became afraid of acting, of doing anything; his life became a hell. And at that time, a mystic passed through the village. The idiot reached the mystic and told his tragic story, asking, "You help me do something...."

The mystic said, "Who says you are an idiot? You are a very simple, innocent being. Out of your innocence you do things which are going to be against the ideas of the cunning and the clever.

"You do one thing—I will be coming back on the same route within a month, so I can check whether it works or not—I will tell you a simple secret. From tomorrow morning, you become assertive, aggressive: Somebody says, 'What a beautiful sunrise' and you immediately jump in and tell him, 'What is there? What beauty are you talking about? What is beauty? Define it! I have seen many sunrises like this; it is just a mediocre sunrise—what is special in it? It happens every day.' And nobody can define beauty, nobody can prove that the sunrise is beautiful. There is no argument, there is no way.

"Somebody is saying, 'Look at that woman, how beautiful she is!' Immediately jump in. You just watch, wherever anybody is making a positive statement about higher values which cannot be proved, you ask for proof: 'What do you mean by calling that ordinary woman, who is not even homely... what beauty is in her? Where is it?—in her eyes, in her nose, in her hair? Where is the beauty? You have to clearly define it, and point to where it is!'" Now, beauty is not something that can be pinpointed.

After one month when the mystic returned, the idiot had become by that time the wisest man in the village. Somebody would say, "That is a holy book," and he would immediately ask, "What do you mean by holy, and what is holy in this book? The paper used is holy, or the ink used is holy, or the words used are holy? What is holy in it? These are the same words, the same ink, the same paper used in every book—what makes this book holy?" And there was no way to prove....

And people became absolutely afraid in his presence. They would tremble, they would not say anything; the situation was completely reversed.

Before, he used to be afraid; now he was never afraid. And nobody even asked a question of him...because the mystic had said, "If somebody asks a question, never answer, but ask a counter-question—because your answer can be criticized; don't be caught in that thing. Just ask a counter-question. Ask, 'What do you mean by this question? Explain each single word and its meaning.' And harass him so much that even an ordinary sentence becomes a puzzle."

The mystic came; the idiot touched his feet and said, "Your strategy worked. Now I am the wisest man in this village."

He said, "Don't be worried—continue. You will be the wisest man in the whole surrounding area, as far as your name can reach! People will start coming to you just to have your blessings."

A small story, but with great significance. It says how even an idiot, by using negativity, can become wise.

But that is not true wisdom. True wisdom is always positive. True wisdom is always arising out of a yes, out of love, out of gratitude towards existence. True wisdom knows no "no." It does not have any contact with negative attitudes and approaches.

You are perfectly right. Just don't remain silent. Bring your silence into songs, bring your experience into expressions. Say to the world what you have known, without fear.

The last thing to be remembered:

The negative person is always restless, because he has nothing; he is empty, he is angry, he is unfulfilled. Out of his unfulfillment, angriness, emptiness, he becomes more and more revengeful, violent. The positive person, the person who has experienced something, becomes calm and quiet. Naturally, he has no need to assert. He has no need to say anything; he is so deeply fulfilled that he does not want to waste his breath unnecessarily fighting. He simply remains settled in his own center.

And this settlement becomes more and more and more and more—to a point that he completely forgets. Not only that he forgets misery, he forgets blissfulness—he becomes so accustomed to bliss...he breathes bliss in and out, day in, day out. It becomes simply his very being; he forgets that he is blissful, that he is experiencing ecstasy. These are just as natural to him as breathing or heartbeats.

Before it happens, you should make an effort—just out of compassion—to show the way to others. They are all groping in darkness; they want some door to open. They are tired of their chains and their handcuffs, and they want somebody to help them to be freed, somebody to say to them that "Yes, there is freedom." They have become so suspicious—perhaps there is nothing like freedom, nothing like blissfulness, nothing like ecstasy. And these negative people go on telling them that these are all imaginations, these are all hypnotic trances; these are not realities. But their innermost beings are thirsty, although their minds are filled and distracted and corrupted by the negative people.

Those who experience something that can be a valuable assurance and encouragement to anybody, anywhere—so that his hope arises again that some window can be opened, that there are doors which he has missed; that he has listened to wrong people, that he has been under the impact of negative darkness and he has not opened his eyes to the positive light—before you become completely satisfied, you have to help people.

You can do it only before you become so settled that you forget at all that you are blissful. Bliss can be experienced only in contrast to misery, and if you have been blissful for years, you have forgotten misery, how it used to be; now bliss has become your only experience. The gap—when you are dropping the misery and moving towards bliss, when you have seen the star for the first time—that is the moment when you should express yourself... "Nobody needs to be a pessimist, nobody needs to drop his hopes. I have seen the star."

But it has to be done quickly, when you see it. When you become the star yourself, then it will be too late. You will not be able to say anything; even the desire to communicate will disappear.

I have heard the pope died, and went to heaven. Saint Peter asked him whom among the saints he would like to meet. "Saint Mary, the mother of Jesus Christ," said the pope.

Saint Peter leads him into a palatial hall. There in a far corner sits an old Jewish lady. The pope approaches her reverently, and sinks to his knees: "Oh, holy mother of God," he says, "all my life on earth I have been looking forward to this blessed moment. There is one question I want to ask you: What was it like to give birth to our Lord Jesus Christ?" The old lady wags her head and smiles. "Well, actually we wanted a girl," she said.

The mother of Jesus Christ is bound to become accustomed to Jesus Christ—he is nothing special to her, her own son. She is disappointed, because they wanted a daughter and they have got a son who is a troublemaker! Because of him, they are condemned, and because of him, in their old age they have to go through great anguish and suffering because he is crucified.

When all the disciples had escaped, the mother was sitting there underneath the cross where Jesus was crucified, crying and weeping. And she must have been thinking it would have been better if a girl had been born. A son—and him too, a son who gets crucified in her old age. And he was so young, only thirty-three. He has given his parents nothing but anxiety. To the pope it is one thing—Jesus Christ is God—but to the old Jewish lady, the mother of Jesus, he was just a troublemaker, unnecessarily disturbing the peace, unnecessarily leaving them in their old age in immense misery because of the crucifixion.

If Jesus Christ is born to you, you will become accustomed. If bliss is born in your being, you will become accustomed. Before you become accustomed, spread the good news as far and wide as possible. There are millions of thirsty people—under the impact of negative, sensational, articulate people, they are suffering in a kind of limbo. They hear only the negative side of things. Naturally they become suspicious of whether any positive side exists at all, or if they are unnecessarily running after shadows and phantoms—because all these clever people are writing against the possibility.

For the new humanity, millions of changes are going to happen. One of the most major changes will be that the positive person has to become articulate. He has to say to the world what he is experiencing, without any fear, without any embarrassment, without any suspicions that it may be imagination. Even if it is imagination, it may do good.

But it is not imagination. You cannot imagine spiritual experiences; you don't have any notion what they are. Unless you know them, there is no way of imagining them, and when you have known them, there is no question of imagination.

The people in the world are in immense need of a few articulate, positive, assertive individuals. Not only their words will be helpful, but their presence—because their words can only be supported by their presence, by their actions, by their responses. There is no other kind of evidence. If people see that you are really living peace, that your life is a song of silence and each of your actions shows it, we can change the whole negative and sick psychology of man.

Otherwise...these negative people have been predominant all through history—because it is very easy to be negative, anybody can do it. Anybody can say, even to Gautam Buddha, that "Whatever you are saying is all nonsense." And even a man like Gautam Buddha cannot produce any evidence of his enlightenment. If the person is adamant, stubborn, closed, there is no way.

Buddha can help the person if he is open, vulnerable, receptive, ready to feel Buddha's presence, ready to feel his fragrance, ready to become part of his silence. But most of the people in the world are living under the impact of negative people. This impact has created such an unconscious state... people go on falling more and more into unconsciousness, into darkness.

Sometimes I think that the Eastern idea has some psychological significance. It may not be true factually and historically, but psychologically...nobody has explored the idea. Just as Charles Darwin proposed the idea of evolution, the East has believed for thousands of years in a contrary idea of involution, not evolution; that man is not growing higher, but falling lower; that the first golden age was in the very beginning.

It is worth understanding the whole idea as a psychological interpretation—not as history, not as science, but as psychology.

The first age, according to the Eastern mystics is called *satyuga*, the age of truth, the golden age. In a way we can see that each man passes through that golden age again when he is a child. When the whole humanity was in its childhood, then the idea becomes very relevant. Children have to learn to speak lies; otherwise, they simply speak the truth, without any learning. Truth is not to be learned, it is just out of your innocence.

Lying needs learning, cleverness, cunningness, calculativeness.

Truth needs only innocence.

So the first age in the Eastern calculation was *satyuga*, the age of truth. They have called it "the golden age." Their description is tremendously significant. Describing satyuga they say it was like a table with four legs, absolutely balanced. Satyuga had four legs, which kept it absolutely balanced. Then things started falling down.

The theory is exactly against Charles Darwin—I call it "involution." One leg dropped. The table became very unbalanced; life became unbalanced. Things were no longer the same as they had been—peaceful, silent, tranquil. With three legs, all balance was lost—but still, the table can be converted into a tripod. A tripod has three legs; some balance is still possible. This second age is called *treta*, because of three legs—*treta* means three. The English word 'three' comes from the Sanskrit root, *tre*, and *treta* also comes from the same root. Life was no longer golden. Innocence was lost—that was the leg that was missing—people became more clever, more cunning.

Then as days went by, things went down more. The third age is called *dwapar*. One more leg dropped; only two legs remained. All balance was lost. *Dwapar* is the same as the English word two. *Dwapar* comes from the Sanskrit root, *dwa*. *Dwa* has moved through many languages, reaching a few languages as *twa*...and by the time it reached the English language, it became two. But it is the same word. Life became ugly, more barbarous, with more exploitation, more negativity.

And we are in the fourth—one leg has fallen again; now we are standing only on one leg. The fourth is called *kaliyuga*, the age of darkness. And it seems certainly true that we are living in an age of darkness and unconsciousness. We are preparing for our own suicide—what more unconsciousness can there be? The future seems to be absolutely meaningless. It seems that every day the end of life is coming closer; the night goes on becoming darker and darker.

Even small children have been found in thousands taking drugs; it is no longer the new generation, it is no longer young people—school kids are taking drugs. School kids have been found murdering other children, school kids have been found raping girls—and not as an exception. In America they had a survey, and they could not believe...the government tried hard to repress it, not to let it be known to the world, but it leaked out.

The most advanced nation, most powerful, most scientifically, technologically advanced, is going through the darkest period in the whole of human history.

This unconsciousness can be broken only if the people whose life has become meditation, whose life has become a pure love, whose life has become a compassion, start waking up other sleeping people: "It is time—get ready. As the night becomes darker, the dawn is closer, but if you go on sleeping, dawn or no dawn, your night continues. Your eyes are closed, your darkness continues."

Otherwise, a new dawn for the whole human race, a new innocence, a new childhood, a new *satyuga*—the age of truth—a new golden age is possible. But the positive people have to take the bold step of expressing themselves. They have not been doing that for the whole of history. They have enjoyed their experience, and they have thought their work was finished.

I want you to remember always:

When you have something to share, don't stop there; share it. Humanity is in need, as it has never been in need, of people who can create new hope for a new dawn.

A Jew comes to an inn, very late at night, and is forced to share a room with a Russian officer. Not wanting to meet him, he asks the innkeeper to wake him up very early in the morning because he has to catch the first train.

The Jew undresses and goes to bed, and is awakened by the innkeeper when it is still dark outside. He dresses quickly and goes out, and to his surprise, all the soldiers salute him. When he mounts the train he looks at the mirror and realizes he is wearing a uniform. "Damn the innkeeper," cries the Jew. "He woke up the wrong man!"

Okay, Maneesha?

Yes, Osho.

4

YOU FOOL AROUND—THEN
LEARN THE LESSON

Up to a point every stupidity is allowed, but only up to a point. If you go on doing the same thing again and again, then stupidity becomes your second nature; then to get out of it is almost impossible.

Beloved Osho,

Would You say something to us about wisdom?

Raso, wisdom is one of the most misunderstood words in any of the languages of the world. Mostly, the misunderstanding has arisen because of the word 'knowledge'. People think both are identical, synonymous. In reality, they are just the opposite of each other.

The knowledgeable man is not the wise man; the knowledgeable man is simply covering up his ignorance by collecting all kinds of information from the outside. His scholarship is great, his information is vast, his memory may be very rich, but he is still not wise—because wisdom has nothing to do with scholarship, nothing to do with scriptures, nothing to do with memory either. Wisdom is the name of pure intelligence. It is the spontaneous flowering of your being.

Knowledge comes from outside.

Wisdom comes from your innermost core.

Knowledge is always borrowed; wisdom is never borrowed. Neither can you take it from anybody, nor can you give it to anybody.

The English word 'education' will help you to understand the distinction. It comes from a root which means drawing out, just the way you draw water out of a well. Education is only an opportunity, a supportive background, where whatever is your potential can be drawn out; whatever is in the form of a seed in you starts growing and comes to blossom.

Wisdom is the spring of your innermost being; it is transformation, not information. But in the name of education, whatever has been happening in the world for centuries is just the opposite. Your intelligence is not drawn out the way water is drawn out from a well, but information is poured in from the outside, just the way it is poured into a computer. The whole education makes you knowledgeable. And the more knowledge gathers, layer upon layer, the less is the possibility for your own being to find a way to grow. The whole space is taken by borrowed junk; wisdom gets suffocated and dies a very early death.

It is strange that even in the twentieth century when we think we have become very cultured, cultivated, educated, evolved, education is still the same as it was in the most primitive times; it is still doing the same act of turning everybody into a robot, into a mechanical memory system. It does not sharpen your intelligence, it makes you only clever enough to remember things.

But remembering is not knowing. Knowing is possible only through meditation.

Meditation is just emptying out all that is rubbish in you, all that is borrowed, all that has been fed into you, and making you again an innocent child who knows nothing. If one can come to this state of not knowing, in this spaciousness of not knowing, something spontaneously starts growing within. It does not come from outside, it comes from the innermost life sources, from your very roots. It brings beautiful flowers. That's why it is possible for a Jesus or a Kabir or a Raidas—people who are uneducated, uncultured. Jesus is the son of a carpenter, Kabir is an orphan— nobody knows whether he is a Hindu or a Mohammedan; he remained his whole life a poor weaver. Raidas is a shoemaker. All three came from the world's most exploited people, the most humiliated, almost reduced into a subhuman species. But they have wisdom. They know nothing of scriptures, but each of their words is pure twenty-four karat gold. Each of their breaths brings the divine into the world. Each of their heartbeats is the heartbeat of the universe itself. They know without knowledge; they understand directly without any mediators.

It happened.... One great Christian missionary who was trying to convert the Japanese people to Christianity went to a great Zen master. He collected information about the man—he was well known far and wide; even the emperor of Japan used to come to touch his feet.

The missionary was puzzled because the Zen master was uneducated, a villager. He thought, "It is a great opportunity to convert this Zen master into a Christian. It won't be difficult; he cannot argue, he knows nothing of logic, he knows nothing of theology, he has not heard anything about philosophy—he cannot resist, he cannot oppose me. I just have to go to him and read a few words of Jesus."

He had chosen the most beautiful part, the Sermon on the Mount. He started asking the permission of the Zen master, "I also have a master and I would like you to listen to a few of his words; I want to know your opinion about it."

He had read only two or three lines and the Zen master said, "Stop! Whoever has said these lines will become enlightened in the next life. Don't waste my time and don't waste your time." The missionary was simply shocked; he had never thought that this would be the response.

The Zen master said, "Don't look shocked, I am being very compassionate. It is not absolutely certain that in the next life he will become enlightened. I am simply consoling you. Most probably he will become...he is a *bodhisattva*, but it is a question of time; no one can predict when a bodhisattva will become a buddha."

The difference is that a bodhisattva means in essence, a buddha, in potentiality a buddha, but not in actuality; just the seed is there. So the possibility is there any day—the seed finds the right soil and the spring comes, and the sprouts start growing out of the seed—but nobody can predict when.

As the missionary was returning, very angry, barely repressing his violent mood—the Zen master said, "Listen, a bodhisattva is nothing special; everybody is a bodhisattva. Everybody is, in essence, a buddha; it is only a question of time. When you realize your essence, you become a buddha. You are also a bodhisattva. The essence of wisdom is lying dormant in every being; you bring it with yourself, it is your self-nature."

Knowledge is nurture, not nature, but millions of people around the world live their whole life under the misunderstanding that knowledge is wisdom. If knowledge was wisdom, then great scholars, professors, Ph.D.'s, D.Litt.'s—all would have become enlightened. But it is very strange that the people who have become enlightened come not from the professional scholars but from very innocent groups. Carpenters are not scholars; nor are weavers, nor are shoemakers, nor are potters, but they all have given enlightened people to the world. Their wisdom was, and even is today, as fresh as the morning dewdrops.

Wisdom never grows old.

Knowledge is always old, it is never fresh. It is being passed from one generation to another generation; it has been going on from one hand into another hand. Wisdom, everybody has to find for himself.

Wisdom is an individual search and its fulfillment. Its beginning is to ask the question, "Who am I?" and its end is to find who is residing in you as your life, as your consciousness. And the moment you have known your being, you have become aware of your immortality.

The Upanishads say, *Amritasya putrah*: you are all sons and daughters of immortality. To know it firsthand, not by repeating the Upanishads but to know it by your own experience, is wisdom.

A Gautam Buddha, a Mahavira, are people of wisdom because they have come face to face with their own reality. What they are saying is not within quotation marks, it is not a repetition of any scripture. What they are saying is on their own authority.

Wisdom is its own authority; it is self-evident, it needs no support from the past.

Knowledge never transforms anybody, it simply burdens you. It may give you respectability, honor, prestige, but it will not make you aware of yourself; you will not know who you are. You may remain a Christian, you may remain a Hindu, you may remain a Buddhist, you may remain a Mohammedan, just because the older generation—your parents, your teachers, your priests—have burdened you, conditioned you, fed you with all kinds of traditional knowledge.

But wisdom, nobody can impart to anybody else. That's its beauty and that's its grandeur. You can find it yourself, but it will be always firsthand—young and fresh and alive. Knowledge is always dead; it stinks of death. Wisdom is fragrant of love, of life, of rejoicings.

James, the eldest son of a respected Hollywood family, walked into his father's study and made a shocking announcement that he now intended to live openly with his gay boyfriend.

"Damn it, James," shouted his father, "our family came over with Columbus and the Mayflower; we have never had a scandal like this!"

"But I can't help it, father," said James, "I am so in love with him."

"But for God's sake, son", shouted his father, "he is Catholic!"

This is knowledge. He is not worried about homosexuality, he is worried that "he is Catholic and you are not Catholic."

The knowledgeable person can be found always acting foolishly, because all the knowledge is just superficial. Deep down he is just the old idiot. A donkey loaded with holy scriptures does not become a holy donkey; he remains a poor donkey. Whether he is loaded with holy scriptures or loaded with unholy bricks, it doesn't matter—he is simply loaded, he is carrying a burden. He will always act according to his understanding.

The man of knowledge is not the man of understanding. His behavior, his actions, will show his foolishness. Yes, he can give a good lecture, he can write a great treatise, he can be a great theoretician, but in actual life, in existential situations, his responses will be of a dead and ignorant man, because his ignorance has not gone anywhere—it is simply repressed under knowledge. And whenever there is a new situation for which he has not collected information ahead, for which he has not done his homework, he is bound to respond from his ignorance. There is no other way, no alternative possible for him.

The wise man is in a totally different situation: he is not knowledgeable, he is utterly innocent and silent, but he has a clarity of vision. His eyes are without the dust of knowledge; he can see clearly and directly and immediately and spontaneously. He is always here and now with his total presence, with his full, flowering consciousness. He will act out of this consciousness, his action will show his wisdom.

It happened once: Gautam Buddha is passing on the road by the side of a village. The village consists of brahmins, scholars, pundits; they are absolutely against Buddha. The knowledgeable people will always be against the wise man because he is a danger to their whole investment. They surround Gautam Buddha and start abusing him, "You are corrupting people's minds, you are corrupting the youth, you are destroying people's morality." The same accusations....

The knowledgeable people have not been knowledgeable enough even to find some new accusations—just the old accusations against Socrates, against Gautam Buddha, against Mahavira, against Jesus, against Baal Shem, against anybody who seems to be dangerous to their knowledge. Because he has something really valuable and alive, in comparison to him, the knowledgeable look so poor. It hurts the ego of the knowledgeable.

Buddha stood there silently, listening very attentively, as if they were saying something very significant. They were abusing him as badly as possible. They were misbehaving, mistreating an innocent man who had not done any harm to them. Even Buddha's followers who were with him started losing patience, but before

Buddha they could not do anything; otherwise they would have put these people right. They were all warriors, because Buddha came from the warrior race; he was the son of a king, and most of his followers in the beginning came from the warrior race, the *chhatriyas*.

Just one disciple of Gautam Buddha would have been enough to finish all those brahmins who were shouting, abusing, using four-letter dirty words against Gautam Buddha.

Listening to them for a time, Gautam Buddha said, "I have a question to ask you. Before I ask the question, I have to ask your permission...because I will not be able to give more time to you today. I have to reach to the other village; people must be waiting for me. But if you have something more to say, something more to convey, I will make a point of it that when I return, I will return on the same route and I will inform you ahead so you can be prepared. And then I can stay as long as you want."

One of the men from the crowd said, "It seems strange, we are not conveying any message to you, we are simply abusing you— and it seems you are not affected at all."

Gautam Buddha smiled and said, "If you want me to be affected, then you have come too late; if you had come to me ten years before, all of you would have been dead by now. But now it is too late—now it does not matter to me, and that's what I was going to tell you.

"In the village that I passed before coming to your village, people had come with sweets, flowers, to welcome me. But I said to them, 'We have taken our one meal—because only one meal is allowed to us by our discipline, and we are not allowed to carry food with us. So we are sorry—we are immensely grateful, thankful; we can see your love and your honor, but we are sorry— you will have to take your sweets, your flowers back.' I want to ask you," he said to the crowd, "what should they have done with the sweets and the flowers?"

One of the men said, "Is that a great question? They should have distributed the sweets in the village; they would have enjoyed eating them."

Buddha said, "You are right. Now, what will you do? You have brought all kinds of ugly words. I don't take them, and without my taking them, you cannot give them to me. You will have to take them back; just the way the other village people had to take their sweets back, you will have to take your presents back that you had brought to me. We don't take presents—you will have to take them. What will you do?"

They looked at each other. Buddha said, "Simply do the same thing: distribute them to each other and enjoy."

Wisdom acts in a fresh way.

Buddha turned to his disciples and said, "Remember, unless you take somebody's insult, you are not insulted. You are insulted only when you take it, you are humiliated only when you accept it. If you don't accept it, the person has to take it back; there is no way for him to give it to you. But I am not at all concerned with the people, I am concerned with you, because although you are standing silently behind me, I can feel the vibe of your anger.

"I can forgive those people because they are knowledgeable but ignorant. I cannot forgive you because you are meditators, and anger is not expected from you. Whatever the situation may be, you have to remain centered and silent, and radiate your meditation. Use the opportunity to radiate your fragrance.

"You have failed in a beautiful situation. These people had created such a beautiful situation—you should be thankful to them. They gave you a chance to test your meditation, how wise you have become. But you started getting angry and hot. Even I started feeling your heat and your vibration all around, although you were keeping hold of yourselves. But subtle vibrations I have always felt—your peace and your silence and your love and your gratitude—and I could see the whole climate changing. I could feel as if suddenly the coolness had disappeared and there was a certain heat, which does not show your depth in wisdom.

"Remember next time, perhaps in the same village when we return...if these people invite us, we will have another chance. Next time remember, wisdom cannot be disturbed. Knowledge has no depth—it can be disturbed very easily."

Raso, your question is, "Would you say something to us about wisdom?" Everything that I am saying to you is about wisdom. The question may be about anything, it doesn't matter; whatever I am saying, I am saying about wisdom.

Your questions go on differing, but my answer, if you listen correctly, is always the same. The reference changes, the context changes, my words change with your question, but whatever I am saying is nothing but expressing different aspects of wisdom.

Beloved Osho,

What is needed for me to make the next jump? Listening to Your words for the last nine years does not appear to bridge the gap, and my experience of silence hasn't either. Where and how can I meet You and dissolve into all that is?

Deva Arpana, the question that you are asking is very simple and yet very complex at the same time. Simple, because although you have been hearing me for nine years, you have not heard a single word.

There is a hearing and there is a listening.

Hearing is simply possible for everybody, because you have ears. Listening is a totally different discipline. When you are hearing your mind is doing a thousand and one things. In that marketplace of the mind, where so much is going on, whatever you hear is lost or mixed with other thoughts, or is interpreted according to your old prejudices. But one thing is certain, you don't hear that which has been said. To be able to hear that, you need a silent mind.

I don't mean that you have to agree with me; there is no question of agreeing or disagreeing—I am simply trying to make the difference clear. You have first to listen, then it is up to you to agree or not agree. But first listen clearly to what is being said, and that is possible only if your mind is in silence.

If your mind is going with thousands of thoughts—relevant, irrelevant—you may hear and yet you will not listen. That's why I say your question is simple in a way and yet complex in another, because it raises the whole question of meditation, how to be in a state of meditation—because only a meditator can listen. Mind is incapable of listening.

Researches in depth psychology have come to very strange conclusions. One of the strangest conclusions is that although it has always been thought that the mind is the medium to connect you with the world—it is a bridge, a mediator, a window—the researchers have found that this is not the case. Mind is a barrier, not a bridge; it is a window, but a closed window not an open window. It is a censor for whatever passes in front of you. And the most surprising fact for the researchers has been that ninety-eight percent of what you hear is not allowed in; only two percent reaches to you—that too, in a distorted form.

If there are five hundred people here, that means there are five hundred versions of what I am saying. If you are asked afterwards to give a report in short of what I have said, you will find five hundred different reports contradicting each other. They were all eyewitnesses; they were all present here!

It happened: one English historian, Edmund Burke, was writing a world history and he was very ambitious. He wanted to make a complete history of the world—from the very beginning, when life started as a fish in the ocean—up to now; the whole world, whatever has happened... And he had devoted almost his whole life to collecting all kinds of facts and figures.

One afternoon he heard a shot behind his house. He ran— there was a crowd—a man was lying...he had been shot. He was not yet dead, but he would die at any moment, so much blood had gone out of his body. And there was a crowd—they were all eyewitnesses. In front of them, the man had been shot and the murderer had escaped.

Edmund Burke enquired from different people and he found different versions of what had happened. They were all eyewitnesses, and their descriptions of the happening were so different. Many were so contradictory that he could not believe it was possible. And then a great question arose in his mind, "What am I doing? I am writing the history of the world from the times when life arose in the ocean as fish, and then all the transformations of life up to the man of today, and I cannot figure it out—just behind my house I have heard a shot, eyewitnesses are present, and yet I cannot figure out what has happened. Of what value is my history?"

He dropped the whole project. He never looked again at all the collected material for which he had wasted almost his whole life. Many of his friends said, "This is not right—just because of a small incident."

He said, "It is not a small incident. It shows that all that I am writing is only my prejudice, my opinion about something for which I don't have any eyewitnesses. And even if I had eyewitnesses, it would be of no use. Something happens behind my home; I hear the sound of a shot, I run there in time—the man is dying, the crowd is standing...and everybody has a different story to tell! Now, what can I say about Confucius? What can I say about Moses? What can I say about Krishna?—whether these people ever existed or not?"

No, history is simply not possible. And it is true, you can see it. For three hundred years this country was under the slavery of Britain. British historians have written about the last three hundred years' history, and Indian historians have also written...and they don't agree on any point. The rulers have their own opinion, their own prejudice; the ruled have their own opinion, their own prejudice. How can they agree? Who is going to decide who is right? There is no third party which is neutral.

You have been here, Arpana, for nine years, but you have not been able to hear. And you are asking, "What is needed for me to make the next jump?"

What next jump? Where is the *first* jump? You have not taken even the first step. You are exactly where you were nine years before. You may be going round and round in the same place with the same mind, with the same prejudice....

Ask for the first step. And the first step will be: learn to listen. You have already accepted the idea: "Listening to your words for the last nine years"...you have taken it for granted that you are capable of listening. Nobody is capable of listening without going through a certain discipline. Yes, you can hear, but don't make them synonymous.

I have heard.... A Baptist, a Presbyterian, a Methodist and a Catholic sat down to dinner. As soon as grace was said, a very large fish was served up. The Catholic immediately rose and helped himself to a good third of the fish, head included. Looking at the others, he pompously announced, "The pope is the head of the church." Naturally, being a Catholic, he is entitled to take the head of the fish; that's what his understanding of religion is.

The Methodist wasted no time and reached across the table, helping himself to another third of the fish, including the tail. Chin high in the air, he said, "The end crowns the work."

The Presbyterian quickly removed the last of the fish, saying, "Truth lies between the two extremes."

The Baptist looked down at the empty plate and, faced with the prospect of a meager dinner, grabbed the glass of water and threw it in the faces of all the three and shouted, "I baptize you in the name of the Lord!"

Everybody is doing his own religion. The Baptist is baptizing. The Presbyterian who believes in the golden mean—the middle way, always remaining in the middle, avoiding the extremes—takes the middle part of the fish. The Catholic takes the head, because the pope is the head of the church, and the Methodist takes the tail and announces that the end crowns the work.

This is almost the situation of everybody. Your religion is your interpretation, your convenience, your comfort. What you hear, you hear only selectively—whatever suits your purpose. If you are sitting here with a predetermined mind, that you know already what is right and what is wrong, you cannot listen.

So the first step for you will be, Arpana, to drop this idea, which you have taken for granted, that you have been listening. If you had been listening for nine years, you would have gone through such a great transformation that you would not have been able to recognize yourself, how much you have changed. But you have not changed at all. That is absolute evidence that you have not listened at all.

So the first step is, start meditating and create the space of silence, so that when you sit here you can really be available to me—not holding anything back—so that I can reach to your heart. But if you remain closed, there is no way.

I cannot interfere in your being unless you invite me. Without your invitation and your openness and receptivity, interfering with your life is against the very fundamental rights of every human being. Everybody should be left alone in his individuality. Unless you invite me, I will stand at the door and wait for you; I will not even knock at your door, because even if I knock you may open the door unwillingly. It will be pointless—you will still be resistant.

If you are waiting for me with open doors and your eyes are looking far away in the distance, waiting for me...and as I come closer to you—as you start hearing my footsteps—you rejoice, then there is a possibility of communion. Then I can say something. Or it may not even need to be said...just being in my presence may be enough—something may start changing within you, without anything being said.

This is one of the paradoxes of existence: you sit here for nine years, hearing, and you don't hear a word. And I am saying to you, "Sit here silently, there is no need even for me to say anything and you will hear it. You will hear the message, because the message is of silence, it does not consist of words."

_ Arpana, forget all those nine years, they have gone down the drain. Begin afresh. This is your first day; count from today. Never mention again those nine years, but make a change. And I am not asking much, I am simply asking, "Be silent." But you cannot be silent unless you are going through meditations.

It is a whole strategy—you are doing meditations of different kinds because one never knows which one is going to suit you. People are different, that's why there are different kinds of meditations. And I have chosen the most fundamental types, so one is bound to suit you. That which suits you, that which brings joy to your heart, a dance to your feet, go deeper into it. If you feel that there are some psychological problems which are hindering you in entering meditation, there are groups in which, under expert guidance, you can drop your psychological problems.

After you have done all this then sitting with me in silence will become possible, and that is an absolute requirement.

Hymie Goldberg was in the middle of a lengthy religious discussion with his psychiatrist.

"Now, do I understand correctly," said the shrink, "that it was your wife who introduced you to religion?"

"Yes, that's correct," said Hymie. "I did not really believe there was a hell until I married her."

That's how we listen.

"Did you hear that Dennis Thatcher died?"

"No, what were his last words?"

"He did not have any, his wife was with him to the end."

Jesus and Moses are playing golf. Jesus hits the ball, which almost falls into the hole, when a rabbit jumps past and swallows the ball. As the rabbit runs off, an eagle appears, catches the rabbit and flies away with it into the sky. A hunter arrives and shoots the eagle, the rabbit falls out of the eagle's claws and as the rabbit hits the ground, the ball shoots out of his mouth and into the hole."

"So, Moses," says Jesus, "now, what do you say?"

"Well, Jesus," says Moses grumpily, "I have actually wanted to ask you all day, do you really want to play golf or do you just want to muck around?"

That's what, Arpana, I want to ask you. Do you really want to listen to me or just to muck around? Nine years is enough. Now, don't waste time. It is not only you, there are people with you in the same boat.

For example, here is a question from Deva Vimal: "Somehow I feel it is not enough now, just to bask in your presence. It is as if you have prepared the soil and it is time for me to do some gardening. But what have I done with this responsibility? I head-trip through my most valuable job, I hurt myself and two beautiful women in a messy triangular something, and I procrastinate about any effort at meditation. Then the other night I heard you say, 'Anything you do out of unawareness will be wrong.' My God, catch twenty-two. Osho, please help me find my courage and method to cut the crap and go within."

On the one hand, you say, "I procrastinate, I make every effort not to meditate," and yet you want to get out of the problems that your mind is creating. And because you are not meditating, the evidence is immediately available.

You say, "Then the other night I heard you say..." You say, "Then..." as if I have said it for the first time, just the other night! My whole life I have been saying only one thing, and that is that anything you do out of unawareness will be wrong and everything that you do out of awareness is right, because awareness is right and unawareness is wrong.

This has been my essential teaching and you have heard it only the other night. And at the same time you don't want to meditate. You yourself are declaring that you avoid making any effort to meditate.

So what do you want? How can you get out of this crap? Your whole life will become more and more a puzzle in which you will get entangled; you will forget all ways of coming back home. Now, what are you doing by creating a "triangular something" with two beautiful women? One woman is enough to make you enlightened—two women are enough to drag you back from enlightenment!

Are you writing a film story or a novel? Because no film story, no novel is possible without a triangular mess. Don't make your life a film, don't make your life a novel. Have you ever heard of any film, any novel, any story, profane or sacred, without there being a triangular mess? Either two men and one woman or two women and one man—that is an absolute necessity for creating the story.

But don't make a story of your life, life is too valuable. Making it a story is destructive. Make it a beautiful growth, a flowering, a celebration, a light unto yourself and for anybody else who is ready to share the light. The night is very dark and the night is very long. Even a single man with a light may be of immense help to millions of people, to bring the dawn closer.

Up to a point every stupidity is allowed, but only up to a point. If you go on doing the same thing again and again, then stupidity becomes your second nature; then to get out of it is almost impossible. It is good that you commit mistakes once—once you become a buffoon, you fool around—then you learn the lesson. And nobody can prevent you from coming out of any triangle in the world. The triangle is not holding you in, you are holding the triangle. And it is so deeply humiliating that people in their old age also continue to play games which they should have left when they were teenagers.

I have heard about three old men, all retired. One was seventy, the other was eighty and the third was ninety, and they used to meet daily, as a routine, in the park every morning. They would sit there in the beautiful garden, in the cool breeze, in the early morning sun, and they would talk about their past golden times, beautiful days, and their present miseries.

One day all three were sitting very silently and very sad. Finally, one man said, "Now it is becoming intolerable, this silence is too heavy. I know we are all in trouble, but sharing with each other the problems, the difficulties, the troubles, the mind will feel a little lighter. I should begin, I should take the initiative and say what my problem is."

So they both said, "Okay."

The man of seventy said, "I feel very embarrassed to say it, but I have to say it; otherwise it will remain on my head and I may not be able even to sleep. A beautiful lady was taking a shower in the bathroom and I was looking through the keyhole and my mother caught me red-handed. I am dying with shame."

The two laughed and consoled him saying, "Don't be foolish, everybody does such things in childhood; there is not much of a problem. We have all done the same things, we have all been caught red-handed. But in childhood...you are a strange fellow, why are you making a fuss about it now?"

The old man of seventy said, "You don't understand at all. It is not an incident from my childhood, it happened just today, this morning!"

They both said, "That is certainly serious. But whatever has happened, has happened, you cannot undo it."

"But your trouble is nothing," said the man of eighty. "You don't know others' troubles, so you start bragging about your trouble. What is great in that? It is natural. A beautiful lady is taking a shower and you are becoming a peeping Tom...that's perfectly okay. What's wrong in it? You are not harming anybody. And your own mother has caught you red-handed; before your mother you are always a child, forget all about it. For the mother you are never a grown-up, so don't make much fuss about it. You don't know what great trouble I am passing through. For almost a week I have not been able to make love to my wife."

The first man said, "That is really a bigger trouble. For a whole week you have not been able to make love to your wife? What is the problem?"

The ninety-year-old man started giggling. He said, "You are an idiot, and you have been your whole life an idiot. Although you are seventy years old, that makes no difference; you are just a seventy-year-old idiot. First ask what he means by making love to his wife."

He said, "What can he mean? It is a well-known fact."

But the old guy insisted, "First ask."

So he asked, "Please tell me, what do you mean by making love?"

He said, "What can I mean? At this age I have found a way of making love to my wife. I take her hand in my hand, I press it three times; then she turns to the other side, I turn to the other side and we fall asleep peacefully. But for seven days continuously, the moment I start trying to find her hand she has said, 'Not today, I have a headache.' These seven days have appeared almost like hundreds of years, and I have not made love to her. And she is so stubborn, she goes on talking about her headache every night. And you think you are having trouble?"

The ninety-year-old man was still giggling and he said, "Listen, now you know what he means by making love. You are both idiots. I knew it from the very beginning what kind of love he makes. But you don't know my trouble, and I am ninety years old—you are just children in comparison to me. I am passing through such bad times, you cannot believe."

They said, "Please tell us."

He said, "What to tell you? Just this morning when I started preparing to make love to my wife, she started shouting and screaming, 'What are you doing, you idiot?' And I said, 'I am not doing anything, I am just trying to make love.'

"She said, 'The whole night! This is the fourth time. Neither you sleep nor do you allow me to sleep—love, love, love....'

"So I said, 'My God, it seems I am losing my memory,' because I was thinking it was the first time. And you think you are having troubles! Now I am worried that whenever I start making love to her, I will be trembling inside...who knows how many times I have already made love? And even if she is lying, I cannot do anything. This is real trouble," he said, "and at the age of ninety—life is ending like a tragedy."

But this is the situation of many people in the world. In different ways you go on making the same mistakes all your life. If you are given another chance to live again, you will make the same mistakes—I can give a guarantee for it—because you don't learn.

This place is a place of learning.

The very meaning of the word 'disciple' is, one who is ready to learn. It is derived from the root which means learning.

This is not a place for everybody, it is not a public place. It is a gathering of disciples, of people who are ready to learn and who are ready to transcend their mistakes; who are ready to transcend their egos; who are ready to transcend their minds and who are ready to explode into a light which is eternal, which is divine, which is another name of God.

Okay, Maneesha?

Yes, Osho.

5

THE ONLY GIFT TO ME: YOUR ENLIGHTENMENT

Just wait with a loving longing, with a welcome in the heart for that great moment, the greatest moment in anybody's life—enlightenment. It comes...it certainly comes. It has never delayed for a single moment. Once you are in the right tuning, it suddenly explodes in you, transforms you. The old man is dead and the new man has arrived.

Beloved Osho,

What is the relationship between enlightenment and the spring of life? Is enlightenment the spring of life?

Chandaram, one basic thing has always to be remembered: not to get involved in questions of intellect. They are pseudo questions, they don't belong to your experience. Mind is tremendously capable of creating questions out of words.

But any question that is created by the mind, out of words, not out of experience, is an exercise in utter futility. You don't know what enlightenment is as an experience, you don't know what the spring of life is as an experience. The question is purely intellectual. It can lead to a great philosophical discussion, but it will not lead to any understanding or any transformation.

Intellect is one of the barriers to reach to the sources of existence. It does not allow you to ask the authentic question. It goes on giving you questions which only appear as questions, but they are not your quest. Of course in a dictionary, enlightenment will mean one thing and spring of life will mean something else.

But here we are not discussing linguistics. And the people who have been writing dictionaries, analyzing language and grammar, are not the people of the path. So the first thing: always remember whether the question is arising from some experiential source or not. If it is not arising from experience, then it is not worth discussing.

Carol, a newlywed, brags that her Romeo is a model husband. We looked up the word 'model' in the dictionary, and found it means "a small imitation of the real thing."

It has been heard that the pope died but was allowed to return to earth to speak to the cardinals. They gathered around him eagerly.

"What is he like?" they clamored. "Is he very old, with a long, white beard, like in all the paintings? Tell us, describe him."

"Well," said the pope, "to start with, she is black."

Knowing is one thing; knowing directly and knowing through books are so different. Sometimes they may appear to be similar, but they are not similar.

I cannot answer your question in terms of intellect, but I can answer it in terms of existential experience.

The spring of life and enlightenment are not the same, although they are deeply related. The spring of life, when it becomes aware of itself, brings you to the experience of enlightenment. In other words, spring of life plus awareness is equal to enlightenment.

The spring of life is available to everybody; otherwise how can you live? Your life is continuously being nourished by the spring of life. The trees are nourished by the spring of life, the flowers blossom...but the juice comes from the spring of life. The whole existence is nothing but a manifestation of the springs of life.

But trees cannot become enlightened—neither can mountains or oceans; neither can animals or birds. They all have the same source of life that you have. But man has a prerogative, a privilege, that he can become aware of his spring of life. This awareness is not possible in any other form in existence. It is man's grandeur, it is his dignity. Existence has given him the most precious opportunity. If he can create awareness, consciousness, more alertness, then his spring of life explodes into a new dimension. The dimension of life becomes the dimension of light, of knowing—knowing the deepest roots of our being in eternity. And the moment we know our roots are eternal, we know our flowers are also going to be eternal.

Enlightenment is a flowering.

The springs of life are seeds; enlightenment is a flower. The seed has come to its ultimate expression—there is no further to go. Springs of life are the lowest rung of the ladder, and enlightenment is the highest rung of the ladder, although the ladder is the same.

The change comes slowly, as you become more aware of who you are, of what life is—not intellectually, not by reading through scriptures, but by reading the only holy scripture: your own being, and bringing your potential to its realization. So that which was hidden in the seed becomes an explosion in the flower, in the fragrance. That fragrance is enlightenment. It comes from the sources of life, but it is not synonymous with it.

The seed is not synonymous with the flower, although the flower comes from the seed. The seed is the womb, but the flower—although connected with the seed, with the womb—is a totally new experience.

Awareness ordinarily is objective. You know others, you know the world, you know the faraway stars. The moment awareness turns inwards and starts knowing itself—in other words, the moment awareness is the object of its own knowing—enlightenment blossoms with all its beauty, with all its immortal glory.

Life is accepted by the scientist, but he is not yet capable of accepting the possibility of enlightenment. Life is accepted by the atheist, but he is also not capable of comprehending the ultimate explosion. Just as for millennia we had no idea that matter is made of small atoms, which are not visible to the eyes...they are so small that if you put one atom upon another atom, and then go on putting one on top of another, you will need one hundred thousand atoms, and then they will be as thick as a human hair. Such a small atom, one hundred thousand times thinner than a human hair, when it explodes, releases so much energy that a city like Hiroshima or Nagasaki disappears within seconds—evaporates.

I have seen a picture sent by a friend from Japan...just looking at the picture, one feels so sad about humanity, so hopeless. The picture is of a small girl, maybe nine years old. She is going from the ground floor to the first story with her bag and books—perhaps to do her homework before she goes to sleep. She is just in the middle of the staircase when the atom bomb falls on Hiroshima.

Just a small atom exploding creates so much energy...you can use it for destruction or you can use it for some creative purpose. Right now the scientists say we have come so far from Hiroshima and Nagasaki—our new nuclear weapons are so great in their energy—that the atom bombs dropped on Nagasaki and Hiroshima look like children's toys.

If matter, in its smallest particle, contains so much energy, can you conceive how much energy may be available in the living cell of human beings?

Enlightenment is the explosion of a living cell. Certainly it is not destructive at all, but it transforms the whole man. In that way, it is destructive. It destroys the old man, it destroys the night, it destroys all that was constituting your personality: your jealousy, your anger, your hate, your lust, your greed—all that is simply finished in a single moment. And the same energy that was involved in jealousy, hate, greed, ambition, and a thousand and one desires, is changed into totally new forms of energy: love, silence, peace, compassion, wisdom—all that is the basic search of life itself.

Life in itself is dormant, it is fast asleep. Enlightenment is absolutely awake. But it is the same energy that was asleep that becomes awake. So they are not synonymous, but they are two extremes of the same energy.

But this, if taken as an intellectual understanding, is not going to help you in any way. It has to become your own experience.

You have to see that light.

You have to see that explosion within your own being.

You have to see the darkness disappearing. You have to see the new dawn of a new life—a life of grace and gratitude, a life of beauty and blessings.

Chandaram, you have to remember, it is very easy to ask questions as mind gymnastics. I am not interested in mind gymnastics because it leads you nowhere; you remain stuck where you are. You only become more burdened with knowledge— knowledge which is meaningless because it is not part of your own experience.

Rabbi Bierstein was asking his congregation to donate money to help build a new synagogue. Suddenly, the town prostitute stood and shouted, "Praise the Lord. I repent. I will give two thousand dollars right now."

"Well, as much as we need funds, I am afraid I cannot accept tainted money," said Bierstein.

"Take it, Rabbi," shouted a man from the back, "after all, it is our money anyway!"

Now, what are these guys doing in a synagogue? Just a formality. They are visiting prostitutes. The prostitute is more authentic. Perhaps the money also belongs to the Rabbi; that's why the man is saying, "It is our money anyway."

Mind has been befooling man for centuries.

After holding mass in Warsaw Cathedral, the pope was giving words of encouragement to a group of devout Poles. One of them asked, "Your Holiness, Poles are such devout Catholics, why was Christ not born in Poland?"

"Don't you understand," said the pope, "that for such a birth, there had to be three wise men and a virgin?"

And where can you find three wise men and a virgin in Poland? You must know the story of Jesus, that he is born out of a virgin, and three wise men come from the East to pay him respect. They are the first to recognize in the small child the possibility of a future enlightened being. They recognized in the seed, the flower.

I recognize in you the seed and the potential of the flower. But if you go on thinking intellectually, you will become a philosopher, a theologian; you will never become a mystic. And unless you become a mystic, you have wasted your life. Such a great opportunity, where you can grow to your greatest height of consciousness, is being wasted in unconscious trivia.

Even if you think about something great, it is only a thought, it never becomes an actual reality in your being.

I would like you to be more existential. I am not an existentialist because that is again falling into the same trap. Existentialist philosophers are not enlightened people. Neither Jean-Paul Sartre is enlightened nor Jaspers, nor Martin Heidegger, nor Marcel, nor Søren Kierkegaard; they are philosophers of existence, they think about existence.

I want you not to be existentialist thinkers; I want you to be existential experiencers. That difference is so great, and makes all the difference—because Jean-Paul Sartre, or Jaspers or other existentialist philosophers live in anguish, in anxiety, in boredom, in despair. They even think that perhaps suicide is the only way out of this mess. These people are not to be categorized with Gautam Buddha or Chuang Tzu or Baal Shem. These people are thinking about existence, just as old philosophers were thinking about God; only the object of thinking has changed, but thinking continues, and thinking can only lead you into a desert.

It is only the experience which leads your life river towards the ultimate merger with the ocean, with the universe, with the life of full awareness. You come back home. You had left the home unconscious, you come back home with consciousness. The circle is complete. Your life has come to fulfillment and contentment. This is the only benediction and this is the only authentic religious path.

Beloved Osho,

If I look at my death, or Your death, one thing I could never forgive myself for is to miss You. I used to think: if life has a purpose, You are the purpose—and if there is a destiny, You are my destiny. Now I see things a little differently. The most beautiful gift my life can give to You is not to worship You or help Your work on this earth. It is not even to love You. Out of Your compassion, as I understand it, the most beautiful gift my life can give to You is my own enlightenment. Please, Osho, give me a technique to prepare my meditation.

R aso, the way your understanding has been growing is perfectly the right way and the right direction. The only thing you should think of is enlightenment. Yes, that is the only gift you can give to me: your enlightenment. Everything else is trivia. So your conclusion has my absolute, categorical approval.

Once you are committed, once you have decided wholeheartedly that enlightenment is the only purpose of being here in the world, of being alive, then a singlepointed awareness—just like an arrow moving towards its target—begins in you.

You are asking for the right meditation. Meditation is a beautiful word; hiding behind it is a very dangerous reality. The dangerous reality is: if you want to be deeply in meditation, you will have to pass through almost a death—the death of the old, the death of all that you used to be, a discontinuity with the past—and a rebirth.

The place where your meditation is going to descend is the place occupied by your mind and your past. So the first and primary work is to clean your interior being of all thoughts. There is no question of choosing to keep the good thoughts in and to throw the bad thoughts out. For a meditator, all thoughts are simply junk; there is no question of good and bad. They all occupy the space inside you, and because of their occupation, your inner being cannot become absolutely silent. So good thoughts are as bad as bad thoughts; don't make any discrimination between them. Throw the baby out with the bath water!

Meditation needs absolute quiet, a silence so deep that nothing stirs within you. Once you understand exactly what meditation means, it is not difficult to attain it. It is our birthright; we are absolutely capable of having it. But you cannot have both: the mind and meditation.

Mind is a disturbance.

Mind is nothing but a normal madness.

You have to go beyond the mind into a space where no thought has ever entered, where no imagination functions, where no dream arises, where you simply are—just a nobody.

It is more an understanding than a discipline. It is not that you have to do much; on the contrary, you don't have to do anything except clearly understand what meditation is. That very understanding will stop the functioning of the mind. That understanding is almost like a master before whom the servants stop quarreling with each other, or even talking with each other; suddenly the master enters the house and there is silence. All the servants start being busy—at least looking like they are busy. Just a moment before, they were all quarreling and fighting and discussing, and nobody was doing anything.

Understanding what meditation is, is inviting the master in. Mind is a servant. The moment the master comes in with all its silence, with all its joy, suddenly the mind falls into absolute silence.

Once you have achieved a meditative space, enlightenment is only a question of time. You cannot force it. You have to be just a waiting, an intense waiting, with a great longing—almost like thirst, hunger, not a word.... It is like the experience of people who have sometimes got lost in a desert. At first, thirst is a word in their mind: "I am feeling thirsty and I am looking for water." But as time goes on, and there is no sign of any oasis—and as far as the eyes can see, there is no possibility of finding water—the thirst goes on spreading all over the body.

From the mind, from just a word, 'thirst', it starts spreading to every cell and fiber of the body. Now it is no longer a word, it is an actual experience. Your every cell—and there are seven million cells in the body—is thirsty. Those cells don't know words, they don't know language, but they know that they need water; otherwise life is going to be finished.

In meditation, the longing becomes just a thirst for enlightenment and a patient awaiting, because it is such a great phenomenon and you are so tiny. Your hands cannot reach it; it is not within your reach. It will come and overwhelm you but you cannot do anything to bring it down to you. You are too small, your energies are too small. But whenever you are really waiting with patience and longing and passion, it comes. In the right moment, it comes. It has always come.

You are asking what meditation will be helpful to you. Raso, all meditations...hundreds of techniques are available, but the essence of all those techniques is the same, just their forms differ. And the essence is contained in the meditation vipassana.

That is the meditation that has made more people in the world enlightened than any other, because it is the very essence. All other meditations have the same essence, but in different forms; something nonessential is also joined with them. But vipassana is pure essence. You cannot drop anything out of it and you cannot add anything to improve it.

Vipassana is such a simple thing that even a small child can do it. In fact, the smallest child can do it better than you, because he is not yet filled with the garbage of the mind; he is still clean and innocent.

Raso, I would suggest vipassana as the technique for you. Vipassana can be done in three ways—you can choose which one suits you the best.

The first is: Awareness of your actions, your body, your mind, your heart. Walking, you should walk with awareness. Moving your hand, you should move with awareness, knowing perfectly that you are moving the hand. You can move it without any consciousness, like a mechanical thing. You are on a morning walk; you can go on walking without being aware of your feet. Be alert of the movements of your body.

While eating, be alert of the movements that are needed for eating. Taking a shower, be alert of the coolness that is coming to you, the water falling on you and the tremendous joy of it.... Just be alert. It should not go on happening in an unconscious state.

And the same about your mind: whatever thought passes on the screen of your mind, just be a watcher. Whatever emotion passes on the screen of your heart, just remain a witness—don't get involved, don't get identified, don't evaluate what is good, what is bad; that is not part of your meditation. Your meditation has to be choiceless awareness.

You will be able one day even to see very subtle moods: how sadness settles in you just like the night is slowly, slowly settling around the world, how suddenly a small thing makes you joyous.

Just be a witness. Don't think, "I am sad." Just know, "There is sadness around me, there is joy around me. I am confronting a certain emotion or a certain mood." But you are always far away: a watcher on the hills, and everything else is going on in the valley. This is one of the ways vipassana can be done.

And for a woman, my feeling is that it is the easiest, because a woman is more alert of her body than a man. It is just her nature. She is more conscious of how she looks, she is more conscious of how she moves, she is more conscious of how she sits; she is always conscious of being graceful. And it is not only a conditioning; it is something natural and biological.

Mothers who have experienced having at least two or three children, start feeling after a certain time whether they are carrying a boy or girl in their womb. The boy starts playing football; he starts kicking here and there, he starts making himself felt—he announces that he is here. The girl remains silent and relaxed; she does not play football, she does not kick, she does not announce. She remains as quiet as possible, as relaxed as possible.

So it is not a question of conditioning, because even in the womb you can see the difference between the boy and the girl. The boy is hectic; he cannot sit in one place. He is all over the place. He wants to do everything, he wants to know everything. The girl behaves in a totally different way.

That's why I say, Raso, it will be easier for you to take vipassana in this first form.

The second form is breathing, becoming aware of breathing. As the breath goes in, your belly starts rising up, and as the breath goes out, your belly starts settling down again. So the second method is to be aware of the belly, its rising and falling. Just the very awareness of the belly rising and falling... And the belly is very close to the life sources because the child is joined with the mother's life through the navel. Behind the navel is his life's source. So when the belly rises up, it is really the life energy, the spring of life that is rising up and falling down with each breath. That too is not difficult, and perhaps may be even easier, because it is a single technique.

In the first, you have to be aware of the body, you have to be aware of the mind, you have to be aware of your emotions, moods. So it has three steps. The second sort has a single step: just the belly, moving up and down. And the result is the same. As you become more aware of the belly, the mind becomes silent, the heart becomes silent, the moods disappear.

And the third is to be aware of the breath at the entrance, when the breath goes in through your nostrils. Feel it at that extreme— the other polarity from the belly—feel it from the nose. The breath going in gives a certain coolness to your nostrils. Then the breath going out...breath going in, breath going out....

That too is possible. It is easier for men than for women. The woman is more aware of the belly. Most men don't even breathe as deep as the belly. Their chest rises up and falls down, because a wrong kind of athletics prevails over the world. Certainly it gives a more beautiful form to the body if your chest is high and your belly is almost non-existent.

Man has chosen to breathe only up to the chest, so the chest becomes bigger and bigger and the belly shrinks down. That appears to him to be more athletic. Around the world, except in Japan, all athletes and teachers of athletes emphasize breathing by filling your lungs, expanding your chest, and pulling the belly in. The ideal is the lion whose chest is big and whose belly is very small. So be like a lion; that has become the rule of athletic gymnasts and the people who have been working with the body.

Japan is the only exception, where they don't care that the chest should be broad and the belly should be pulled in. It needs a certain discipline to pull the belly in; it is not natural. Japan has chosen the natural way; hence you will be surprised to see a Japanese statue of Buddha. That is the way you can immediately discriminate whether the statue is Indian or Japanese. The Indian statues of Gautam Buddha have a very athletic body: the belly is very small and the chest is very broad. But the Japanese Buddha is totally different; his chest is almost silent, because he breathes from the belly, but his belly is bigger. It doesn't look very good because the idea prevalent in the world is the other way round, and it is so old. But breathing from the belly is more natural, more relaxed.

In the night it happens when you sleep: you don't breathe from the chest, you breathe from the belly. That's why the night is such a relaxed experience. After your sleep, in the morning you feel so fresh, so young, because the whole night you were breathing naturally...you were in Japan!

These are the two points: if you are afraid that breathing from the belly and being attentive to its rising and falling will destroy your athletic form...men may be more interested in that athletic form. Then for them it is easier to watch near the nostrils where the breath enters. Watch, and when the breath goes out, watch.

These are the three forms. Any one will do. And if you want to do two forms together, you can do two forms together; then the effort will become more intense. If you want to do all three forms together, you can do all three forms together. Then the process will be quicker. But it all depends on you, whatever feels easy.

Remember: easy is right.

As meditation becomes settled, mind silent, the ego will disappear. You will be there, but there will be no feeling of "I." Then the doors are open. Just wait with a loving longing, with a welcome in the heart for that great moment, the greatest moment in anybody's life—enlightenment.

It comes...it certainly comes. It has never delayed for a single moment. Once you are in the right tuning, it suddenly explodes in you, transforms you. The old man is dead and the new man has arrived.

Big Chief Sitting Bull had been constipated for many moons. So he sent his favorite squaw to the medicine man for help. The medicine man gave the squaw three pills and told her to give them to the chief, and then report back to him the next morning.

The next morning the squaw came back with the message, "Big chief no shit." So the medicine man told her to double the dose.

The next day, she came back with the message, "Big Chief no shit." So again he told her to double the dose.

Again she came back with the same message. This went on for a week, and finally the medicine man told the squaw to give Sitting Bull the whole box.

The next morning, she came back with a very sad expression. "What is wrong, my child?" asked the medicine man. The little squaw looked at him with tears in her eyes and said, "Big Shit, no chief!"

One day it will happen to you, and that will be a great moment. That's what I am calling the right moment.

Okay Maneesha?

Yes, Osho.

6

LETTING ME IN IS FINDING YOURSELF

Decide any way—whichever suits you. If your old mind is a great joy to you, there is no need for me to disturb you; be satisfied with your old mind. But it cannot be the case. If the old mind was right, you would not have been here. You are here in search of something new, in search of something unknown, in search of an alchemical change.

Beloved Osho,

What is the language of enlightenment?

Milarepa, there is no language of enlightenment. There cannot be by the very nature of the phenomenon. Enlightenment happens beyond mind and language is part of the mind. Enlightenment is experienced in utter silence.

If you want to call silence a language, then of course enlightenment has a language which consists of silence, which consists of blissfulness, which consists of ecstasy, which consists of innocence. But this is not the ordinary meaning of language. The ordinary meaning is that words have to be used as a vehicle to convey. Silence cannot be conveyed by words; neither can ecstasy or love or blissfulness. In fact, enlightenment can be seen, can be understood, can be felt, but cannot be heard and cannot be spoken.

I have told you the story: When Gautam Buddha became enlightened, he remained silent for seven days and the whole existence waited breathlessly to hear him, to hear his music, to hear his soundless song, his words coming from the land of the beyond—words of truth...the whole existence was waiting. And those seven days looked like seven centuries.

The story is tremendously beautiful. Up to a certain point it is factual and beyond that it becomes mythological, but by mythological I do not mean it becomes a lie. There are a few truths which can only be expressed through myths. He attained enlightenment, that is a truth; he remained silent for seven days, that is a truth. That the whole existence waited to hear him is a truth, but only for those who had experienced something of enlightenment and who had experienced the waiting existence, not for everybody.

But still it can be understood that existence rejoices whenever somebody becomes enlightened—because it is a part of existence itself that is coming to its highest expression, a part of existence that is becoming an Everest, the highest peak. Naturally, it is existence's crowning glory. It is the very longing of the whole: one day to become enlightened, one day to dispel all unconsciousness and flood the whole existence with consciousness and light...destroy all misery and bring as many flowers of joy as possible.

Beyond this point it becomes pure mythology, but still it has its own significance and its own truth.

The gods in heaven became worried. One thing has to be understood: Buddhism does not believe in a God; neither does Jainism believe in a God, but they believe in gods. They are far more democratic in their concepts than Mohammedanism, Judaism or Christianity—these religions are more fascist. One God, one religion, one holy scripture, one prophet—they are very monopolistic. But Buddhism has a totally different approach, far more democratic, far more human. It conceives millions of gods.

In fact, every being in existence has to become a god one day. When he becomes enlightened, he will be a god. There is no creator as such; the very idea is ugly. If God has created you, you are only puppets; you don't have an individuality of your own, your strings are in the hands of the puppeteer. And if God can create you, he can uncreate you any moment. Neither did he ask you when he created you, nor will he ask you when he destroys you. You are just a victim of a whimsical, dictatorial, fascist God.

According to Buddhism there is no God as a creator, and that brings dignity to every being. You are not puppets, you have an individuality and a freedom and a pride. Nobody can create you, nobody can destroy you; hence another concept has come out of it: nobody can save you except yourself. In Christianity there is the idea of the savior; in Judaism there is the idea of the savior—if there is a God, he can send his messengers, prophets, messiahs to save you. Even liberating yourself is not within your hands. Even your liberation is going to be a sort of slavery—somebody else liberates you. And a liberation that comes from somebody else's hands is not much of a liberation.

Freedom has to be achieved, not to be begged for. Freedom has to be snatched away, not to be prayed for. A freedom that is given to you as a gift out of compassion is not of much value. Hence, in Buddhism there is no savior either. But there are gods— those who have become enlightened before.

Because there is no creation, existence is eternal; it never began and it will never end. This has to be understood. Christianity says that God created the world exactly four thousand and four years before Jesus Christ was born. Now, this is a very simple logic, that anything that begins in time is bound to end in time someday. You cannot have only a beginning without an end. However far away the end may be, there is bound to be an end because there has been a beginning. Hence, in religions where God is a creator, existence cannot have the rejoicing of eternity, timelessness, deathlessness, immortality.

Since eternity, millions of people must have become enlightened; they are all gods. These gods became disturbed when seven days of silence passed after Gautam Buddha's enlightenment, because it rarely happens that a human being becomes enlightened... It is such a rare and unique phenomenon that the very soul of existence waits for it, longs for it, and thousands of years pass and then somebody becomes enlightened. And if Gautam Buddha is not going to speak, if he chooses to remain silent...which is a natural possibility because silence is the only right language for enlightenment. The moment you try to bring it into language it becomes distorted. And the distortion happens on many levels.

First, it becomes distorted when you drag it down from its height, from the peaks, to the dark valleys of the mind. The first distortion happens there. Almost ninety percent of its reality is lost.

Then you speak. The second distortion happens because what you can conceive in the deepest core of your heart is one thing; the moment you bring it into expression as words, that is another thing. You feel great love, but when you say to someone, "I love you," suddenly you realize the word 'love' is too small to express what you are feeling. It seems really embarrassing to use it.

And the third distortion happens when it is heard by somebody else, because he has his own ideas, his own conditionings, his own thoughts, opinions, philosophies, ideologies, prejudices. He will immediately interpret it according to himself. By the time it reaches the person, it is no longer the same thing that had started from the highest peak of your consciousness. It has gone through so many changes that it is altogether something else. So it has happened many times that enlightened people have never spoken. Out of a hundred enlightened people, perhaps one may have chosen to speak.

Gautam Buddha was such a rare human being, so well-cultured, so articulate, that if he chose to remain silent, the world would miss a great opportunity. The gods came down, touched the feet of Gautam Buddha and asked him to speak. "The whole existence is waiting. The trees are waiting, the mountains are waiting, the valleys are waiting, the clouds are waiting, the stars are waiting. Don't frustrate everyone. Don't be so unkind, have some mercy and speak."

But Gautam Buddha had his own argument. He said, "I can understand your compassion, and I would like to speak. For seven days I have been wavering between the two, whether to speak or to not speak, and every argument goes for not speaking. I have not been able to find a single argument in favor of speaking. I am going to be misunderstood, so what is the point when you are going to be misunderstood?—which is absolutely certain. I am going to be condemned; nobody is going to listen to me the way the words of an enlightened man have to be listened to. Listening needs a certain training, a discipline, it is not just hearing.

"And even if somebody understands me, he is not going to take a single step, because every step is dangerous; it is walking on a razor's edge. I am not against speaking, just I cannot see that there is any use, and I have found every argument against it."

The gods looked at each other. What Gautam Buddha was saying was right. They went aside to discuss what to do now. "We cannot say that what he is saying is wrong, but still we would like him to speak. Some way has to be found to convince him." They discussed for a long time and finally they came to a conclusion.

They came back to Gautam Buddha and they said, "We have found just one single, small argument. It is very small in comparison to all the arguments that go against, but still we would like you to consider. Our argument is that you may be misunderstood by ninety-nine percent of the people, but you cannot say that you will be misunderstood by a hundred percent of the people. You have to give at least a little margin—just one percent. And that one percent is not small in this vast universe; that one percent is a big enough portion. Perhaps out of that one percent, very few will be able to follow the path.

"But even if one person in the whole universe becomes enlightened because of your speaking, it is worth it. Enlightenment is such a great experience that even if your whole life's effort can make one person enlightened, you have done great. To ask for more is not right; this is more than enough. And there are a few people—you must be aware, as we are aware— who are just on the borderline. Just a little push, a little encouragement, a little hope and perhaps they will cross the boundary of ignorance, they will cross the boundary of bondage, they will come out of their prisons. You have to speak."

Gautam Buddha closed his eyes and thought for a few moments, and he said, "I cannot deny that much possibility. It is not much but I do understand that all my arguments, howsoever great, are small before the compassion. I will live for at least forty-two years, and if I can make a single individual enlightened I will feel immensely rewarded. I will speak. You can go back unburdened of your worry and concern." And he spoke continuously for forty-two years.

And certainly not one, but nearabout two dozen people became enlightened. But these two dozen people were the people who learned the art of listening, who learned the art of being silent. They did not become enlightened because of what Buddha was saying, they became enlightened because they could feel what Buddha was—his presence, his vibe, his silence, his depth, his height.

These two dozen people were not becoming enlightened just by listening to the words of Gautam Buddha. Those words helped: they helped them to be in the presence of Gautam Buddha, they helped them to understand the beauty ordinary words take when they are used by an enlightened person. Ordinary gestures become so graceful, ordinary eyes become so beautiful, with such depth and meaning. Just the way Buddha walks has a different quality to it, just the way he sleeps has a different significance to it. These were the people who tried to understand not what Gautam Buddha was saying, but what he was being. His being is the only authentic language.

But millions heard him, became knowledgeable. And the day he died, the same day, thirty-two schools sprang up, thirty-two divisions amongst the disciples—because they differed in their interpretations of what Gautam Buddha had said. Every effort was made that they should gather together and compile whatever they had heard from Gautam Buddha, but all their efforts were failures. There are thirty-two versions, so different that one cannot believe how people can hear one person in so many ways.

Even today those thirty-two schools go on quarreling. For twenty-five centuries they have not been able to be reconciled with each other. In fact, they have gone farther and farther away from each other. Now they have become independent philosophies, proposing that "That is what Gautam Buddha has said and everybody else is wrong. This is the holy scripture. Others are just collections by people who don't understand."

It is one of the great problems, Milarepa, that you have raised: "What is the language of enlightenment?" The being of the enlightened person is his language. To be in contact with him, to drop all defenses, to open all the doors of your heart, to allow his love to reach to you, to allow his vibe to become your vibe....

Slowly, slowly, if one is ready, unafraid, then the heart of the disciple starts dancing in the same tune as the master. Something is being transpired which nobody can see. Something has happened; something which has not been said has been heard. Something which is not possible to be brought into words, has been conveyed through silence—just through looking into your eyes, or just holding your hand, or just sitting by your side in silence.

But language as such...there is none.

Grandpa Hymie Goldberg went to see his doctor. "What is the problem?" asked the physician.

"Well, doc," said Hymie, "it is like this: after the first I am very tired; after the second I feel all ill; after the third my heart begins to pound; after the fourth I break out in a cold sweat; after the fifth I am so exhausted I feel I could die."

"Incredible," said the doctor. "How old are you?"

"Seventy-six," replied Grandpa Hymie.

"Well, at seventy-six don't you think you should stop after the first?" said the physician.

"But doctor," said old Hymie, "how can I stop after the first floor, when I live on the fifth?"

Language is not much, even in ordinary life. Rather than giving understanding to each other, it gives many misunderstandings.

Two robbers broke into a bank in a small town. "All right," said the bigger man, "line up! We are gonna rob all the men and rape all the women."

"Wait a second," snapped his partner. "Let's just grab the money and beat it."

"Shut up, and mind your own business," said a little old lady from the back. "The big fellow knows what he is doing."

Language is a very fragile instrument, but it works as far as ordinary life is concerned. It is utilitarian, but the moment you start moving towards the non-utilitarian existence, language starts failing you. For example, in poetry language is not so clear as in prose. Prose is simple to understand. Poetry needs interpretation, and interpretations can be many.

The Hindu holy book *Shrimad Bhagavadgita* has one thousand interpretations. It is great poetry; and the poet takes every license with language. He is allowed; otherwise there would be no difference between prose and poetry. You cannot write a scientific treatise in the form of poetry, and you cannot write a love letter the way you solve a mathematical problem. The love letter has to be poetic; even though it is written in prose its essence is poetry.

Poetry has beauty, but becomes vague. It is difficult to catch hold of it—it becomes more and more elusive. The greater the poetry, the more elusive. You feel something, but you cannot exactly pinpoint what it is, where it is.

It happened.... A professor of literature at London University suddenly stopped when he was teaching about the poetry of a great English poet, Coleridge. Just in the middle of the poem he said, "Forgive me, I cannot be unjust to the poet. I can manage and you will not be able to detect it, but I cannot deceive myself: beyond these lines everything is vague, illusory. I don't understand, myself, exactly what he means. And fortunately, Coleridge lives in my neighborhood so it will not take much time; tomorrow I will come having asked him what he means by these words. So just forgive me for one day."

He must have been a very sincere and honest man; otherwise it is very easy to make up some meaning. And people must have been making up that meaning—other professors before him and after him.

He went that evening to Coleridge and he said, "Forgive me disturbing your peaceful evening, but I had to come because I cannot be insincere; neither can I be unjust to you. I have loved you, respected you. Each of your words is pure gold. But the mystery becomes too much here, in these lines, and I cannot figure out exactly what their meaning is. They seem to contain much, but perhaps too much for my mind to grasp. It will be a great kindness on your part if you can tell me what you mean by these statements."

Coleridge said, "You will have to forgive me because when I wrote them, two men knew the meaning of these lines. Now only one man knows."

The professor said, "Then there is no problem," because he thought that that one man could not be anybody else but Coleridge. Who bothers about the other man, whether he still has the understanding or not?

Coleridge said, "You don't understand. When I wrote these lines, God knew and I knew. Now I don't know, only God knows. If you meet him somewhere, ask him. And if you can find the meaning, please inform me, because whenever I come to this place I become puzzled myself. There is something, there is something great; but because it is great, mind falls short. It has come from beyond the mind."

And a poet is not capable of going beyond the mind. That is the difference between a poet and a mystic: the mystic can go beyond the mind; the poet once in a while finds himself, accidentally, beyond the mind, but it is not his will. It happens once in a while, but not according to his desire. When it happens, he catches as much as he can. He fills himself with the beauty, with the significance, with the joy, as much as he can—pours it into poetry. But it is beyond his willpower. He cannot manage to open the door to the beyond whenever he wants; the breeze comes whenever it wants to come.

When Coleridge died, he left forty thousand poems unfinished. Because the door opened for a moment, he saw something, but by the time he managed to write it, the door had closed. It is almost like lightning—you see the whole place, just a glimpse, and then it is all darkness. You remember a few things, as if seen in a faraway dream. You can write, but it will remain incomplete.

His friends insisted continuously, "Coleridge, what you are doing is not right. Some poem needs only two lines more and it will be complete. And it is a great poem."

But he said always the same thing: "I have tried, but when I look, I can see my words are very ordinary. Although nobody will be able to detect it, I will always know. I cannot deceive myself. These poems will remain incomplete until the beyond opens again, and fills my heart with the song that has left an incomplete impression, so that I can complete it."

He completed only seven poems. Only seven poems have made him one of the greatest poets of the world, for the simple reason that the quantity is not much but the quality is. You may have written seven thousand poems, it makes no difference—they will not come to the height of Coleridge. He is the only man in the whole history of literature who is thought to be a great poet only on the grounds of seven poems.

Rabindranath is thought to be a great poet. He has six thousand poems complete, of great grandeur. Of course you can call him a great poet. But Coleridge's greatness consists of a totally different dimension—his quality.

If this is the situation of the poet, you can understand the situation of the mystic. The poet simply goes just a few steps beyond the mind, and the mystic has gone forever beyond the mind. He lives beyond the mind; he never comes back to the mind. He cannot express his enlightenment in any language. Even if he speaks, he speaks as a device; he speaks to attract the seekers to feel his being, to feel his presence, to be overwhelmed by his fragrance. He is using language only as a trap, because you can understand only language.

But once you start falling in love with somebody, although in the beginning it is only his language, his poetry, his graceful assertions, his mysterious words...slowly, slowly you come closer and closer. Words are forgotten and the person becomes more and more important, his presence becomes more and more tangible. You can almost touch it. His silence slowly starts reaching within you, creating a communion—not a communication.

There is a story about a Sufi mystic, Jalaluddin Rumi, who has been loved by Sufis the most. He is the only Sufi mystic who has been called *Mevlana*: master of masters. And he was certainly a master of masters.

A caravan was passing through the desert, and in a castle in the desert Jalaluddin Rumi had his campus, where seekers from all over the Middle East used to come to see him. The people in the caravan thought, "It is a good place for the night's rest. We and our camels are all tired. And moreover, it is a good chance, just out of curiosity, to see what is happening with this madman, Jalaluddin Rumi, who attracts strange people from faraway countries. And we don't see any point in it. He looks to us a little mad, but they call him a master of masters." So just out of curiosity they stopped under the trees and went into the castle to see what was happening.

Jalaluddin was teaching. His teaching consisted of pure poetry; he would sing a song. They heard his songs—they looked like utterances of a madman: irrelevant, unconnected. Beautiful words, but saying nothing...strange sentences. When you are hearing them you feel great; when later on you think about them you find nothing, your hands are empty. They left in the morning.

When they were returning they again stopped, just out of curiosity: "What is happening now?" Jalaluddin was sitting with closed eyes, and all the disciples were sitting with closed eyes with him. Nobody was saying anything and nobody was hearing anything.

They said, "Now things have gone from bad to worse. Last time at least that madman was saying something which at least looked beautiful—without meaning. But now he is sitting with closed eyes, and all these idiots are sitting with closed eyes. Now there is nothing for us." So they went away.

On their second trip they again passed by the side of the castle, and they again stopped to see how much the madness had progressed. There was only Jalaluddin Rumi sitting, and nobody else.

They said, "So all those idiots are gone. This is strange—very strange progress of the disciples. Where have they disappeared to? They have all left."

Seeing nobody there, they took courage, approached Jalaluddin, and asked him, "It is not good to disturb you, but we cannot resist our temptation to ask—what happened to your disciples?"

Jalaluddin looked at him—the man who was asking—and the crowd behind him, the whole caravan. He said, "I have been watching you. The first time you stopped I was speaking to my disciples, just preparing them so that they can sit in silence with me. The next time you passed, they had become mature enough, they were sitting in silence with me.

"This time you have come, they have all gone to spread the message. They have ripened, they have arrived at the space they had been searching for. Now they have gone to catch hold of other mad people. I will have to begin again when new people come. I will talk, and when they are ready just to enjoy my presence in silence, then I will sit in silence with them. And when they have come so close that their heart and my heart have become one, I will send them to fetch other mad people who are in need of me."

Enlightenment has no language, Milarepa. But enlightenment finds ways, even without language, to convey the essential message. Even language can be used as a device, but it is not a communication of the experienced truth. That communication will happen only in communion.

Everything can be used, and different masters use different things. Jalaluddin Rumi used to dance, and his dance was so infectious that people would start dancing with him. And just by dancing with him, something would start transpiring.

Nanak traveled all over India and outside India—the only great Indian mystic who ever went outside India. And he had only one disciple with him in all these travels. He went to Sri Lanka, he went to Mecca and Medina in Saudi Arabia, far and wide—and he was walking. All that he used to do was just to sit under a tree and his disciple, Mardana, used to play on a certain musical instrument. He would play music and Nanak would sing a song. And there was such beauty in his song, and in the music of Mardana, that even people who did not understand their language would come there and sit close to them.

After the music was finished, Nanak would sit silently. And the people who had become enchanted with the music, without understanding—because it was not their language...a few would leave, but a few would sit because now his silence had also become a tremendous magnetic force.

He was an uneducated man and he used only a villager's language—Punjabi. But he managed to create an impact on almost half of Asia. Without any language, he managed to make disciples. I am reminded of a small but tremendously valuable incident.

Near Lahore there was a campus of Sufi mystics, very famous in those days—five hundred years ago. People used to come from far and wide to Lahore for that mystic gathering.

Nanak also reached there, and he was just taking a bath outside the campus when the chief Sufi heard that he was there. Neither he understood Nanak's language, nor Nanak understood his language; but some way had to be found. He sent one of his disciples with a beautiful cup full of milk, so full that even one more drop of milk could not be contained in it. And he sent that cup of milk to Nanak.

Mardana could not understand: "What is the matter? What are we supposed to do? Is it a gift, is it a welcome?" Nanak laughed and he looked around, found a wildflower, and floated it in the milk. The wildflower was so light that it did not disturb the milk, and nothing came out of the cup. And he gave the signal to the man to take it back.

The man said, "This is strange. I could not understand why this milk has been sent, and now it has become even more mysterious: that strange fellow has put a wildflower in it." He asked the chief Sufi, his master, "Don't keep me in ignorance. Please tell me what the secret of all this is. What is going on?"

The chief mystic said, "I had sent that cup full of milk to tell Nanak, 'Go on to somewhere else; this place is so full of mystics, there is no need of any more mysticism. It is too full, just like this cup. We cannot welcome you; it will be unnecessarily crowding the place. You go somewhere else.' But that man has managed to float a flower in it. He is saying, 'I will be just like this flower in your gathering. I will not occupy any space, I will not be a disturbance in your gathering. I will be just a beautiful flower, floating over your gathering.'"

The Sufi mystic came, touched the feet of Nanak and welcomed him—without language; nothing was said. Nanak remained their guest, every day singing his songs, and the Sufis were dancing, enjoying. And the day he left they were crying. Even the chief mystic was crying. They all came to give him a send-off. Not a single word of language was exchanged—they had no possibility of any communication. But a great communion happened.

Enlightenment has no language, Milarepa, but enlightenment is capable of finding ways of conveying its rejoicings, its blissfulness, its truth, its love, its compassion...all that is great in human experience—the highest peaks of consciousness.

Beloved Osho,

I am experiencing that the more I find my inner child, the more You come into me. When I feel that strongly I panic, slam the door, and rush into my strong, adult mind. I tell myself not to let You take me over. Sometimes I think that letting You in and finding myself are synonymous, which makes me wonder. Am I a hopeless case?

Prabodh Nityo, you are not a hopeless case, but you can turn out to be—you can manage it. You are creating the situation. Just listen to your question: "I am experiencing that the more I find my inner child, the more you come into me." This is the very purpose of your being here, to allow me in. But instead of rejoicing, you say, "When I feel that strongly I panic, slam the door, and rush into my strong, adult mind."

Something great comes to your door—something for which you are longing, something which has brought you here—but when it knocks on your door, you forget all about the fact that you have longed for this moment, perhaps for lives. You "panic, slam the door, and rush into your strong, adult mind." You tell yourself not to let me take you over.

This is just old habit.

This fear comes to everybody.

On the one hand, you want me to transform you. On the other hand, you are afraid of any change. On the one hand, you want to pass through a revolution to become totally new and fresh. On the other hand, the grip of the old is too strong. So as long as your prayers are not heard, everything is okay.

Millions of people are going to the temples, to the churches, to the synagogues, to the mosques, to the gurudwaras, just for a single reason—because there is no God to hear their prayers. If their prayers were heard, nobody would go even close to the temples. Everybody would panic!—for the simple reason that to allow God or to allow the beyond to enter in you is to be possessed of something which is far bigger than you.

You are no longer in possession; you are possessed—possessed of such a tremendous force that unless you are ready to drop your ego, your personality, your separation, you are bound to feel in a terrible shock, scared, and do everything to prevent this overwhelming experience from happening.

"And sometimes," you say, "I think that letting you in and finding myself are synonymous." These must be the times when I am far away from you and there is no fear of being overtaken; when there is no fear that I will hear you; when there is no fear that I am so close that you have to close the doors and run away into your adult mind. But this is far truer...this is what you have asked, you have been asking every moment to happen.

It is exactly the case. Letting me in is finding yourself. In the deepest core, you and I are not separate—nobody is. In the deepest center, we are all one. So whether you allow your own child, your own innocence, or you allow me in, it is the same, it is synonymous. The moments when you feel this are saner moments, but you feel this only when nothing is happening and you are well defended: the doors are closed, you have slammed everything shut, and you are perfectly protected by your adult mind. Then you start thinking again because your mind is not your contentment, your mind is not your peace, your mind is not your god. Your mind is your prison, and you are thinking you are very secure.

When I was in prison in America, in the first jail...because they kept on moving me from one jail to another. In twelve days I had the great experience of being in five jails. Perhaps it is unprecedented—in twelve days, covering five jails! In the first jail, the man in charge was a beautiful old man, and he immediately fell in a kind of deep intimacy with me. He told me, "Here you are absolutely secure."

I said, "That's absolutely true, in a jail certainly one is absolutely secure. Security and jails are synonymous. Outside there are all kinds of dangers—in jail nobody can rob you, nobody can murder you...you are perfectly secure." I said, "You are right, but you don't follow your own advice."

He said, "What do you mean?"

I said, "In America, twenty percent of the presidents have been assassinated. This is the greatest record of assassination in the whole world. Out of five, one president is going to be assassinated."

He said, "I don't follow. What do you mean by bringing in these assassinations of the presidents?"

I said, "You should keep your presidents in jail instead of keeping me in jail. Ronald Reagan needs to be in jail; here he will be absolutely secure. As far as I am concerned, I have lived my whole life outside. And how long will you keep me in jail? You are keeping me in jail illegally, without any arrest warrant. You don't have any evidence of any crime against me. So just a few days' security will not help—again I will be outside.

"And I am of no importance to anybody. I am not a president of a country or a prime minister of a country; I am not a pope of any religion. I don't need any security. Your idea is great. You should suggest to the senate that every president, once he is chosen, should be immediately imprisoned. This way you will save the twenty percent assassinations."

He said, "My God! You are really dangerous. I have heard that you are dangerous...you are! What kind of ideas are you putting into my head? I'm just on the verge of retirement; don't disturb my life."

I said, "It was your idea. And why do you live outside the jail? It is dangerous outside. Just come in and be safe."

He said, "It is very difficult to argue with you. The whole idea is wrong, but you are convincing."

I said, "It is your idea. You told me, 'You are very secure here—rest, don't be disturbed; nobody can disturb you.' I have just been extending your idea to its logical end. If you follow your own advice, don't go home."

He really fell in love with me. For three days I was in his jail—I was in the hospital part of the jail. The nurses told me, "You have changed the whole climate here, because this man, who is in charge of the jail, used to come once in six months or once a year to visit this section. Now that you are here, he comes at least six times a day to meet you. He cannot sit in his office." He used to take me to his office also..."Just come, have a cup of tea in my office and we will discuss something."

I said, "Listen, if the government comes to know, you will be in trouble."

He said, "I don't care because I'm going to be retired soon."

And the world news media wanted to interview me in the jail. He said, "This is unprecedented, but I will allow the world press conference." And he allowed it...in the jail were one hundred journalists: television people, radio people, newspaper people, magazine people, cable television people.

And he said, "I'm going to be retired. They can retire me a little earlier at the most. What else can they do? And there is no prohibition in the jail code saying that no press conference can be held inside the jail. So there is no problem."

I said, "That's perfectly good."

He enjoyed the press conference so much, and whatever I said to the press people. His whole staff was there to listen: the doctor, the nurses, everybody was there. And from the next day on they started bringing their families to see me. I said, "What?" And their children started bringing their autograph books!

The nurses could not find anything for me to sign, but in the newspapers there were many pictures of me, so they started bringing cuttings of photographs from the newspapers: "We will remember that once you have been here for three days. This will be our memory...the most cherished memory. In these three days this place has not been a jail at all."

The nurses were coming even on the day which was their day off. They said, "We will lose that day, but you may go any moment and we don't want to miss any time."

You are worried about security, safety; that if I take you over, or I become your very center, then what is the guarantee of your security and your safety? You are already living in a prison. If I can come within you, I can pull you out of your prison—even from the outside. That's what I am trying to do: to pull you out of your old mind.

You are not a hopeless case, Prabodh Nityo, but if you go on doing this, then it becomes impossible for me to help you in any way. If you panic, if you slam the door and rush into the strong, adult mind behind a protective wall, then you are doing a schizophrenic act: on the one hand you are asking me to come and transform you, and on the other hand when I come to you, you close the door.

Decide any way—whichever suits you. If your old mind is a great joy to you, there is no need for me to disturb you; be satisfied with your old mind. But it cannot be the case. If the old mind was right, you would not have been here. You are here in search of something new, in search of something unknown, in search of an alchemical change. Now gather courage. And it is a question only of a single moment.

Stop slamming doors, and stop running into a defense. I cannot destroy you, I can only destroy that which is not you. I can discover and help you to discover your authentic being. But you are in an absolute misunderstanding.

On his wedding night, the preacher returned to the bedroom from brushing his teeth and found his newlywed lying in bed stark naked, on her back, with her legs spread invitingly.

"Praise the Lord!" cried the preacher. "I expected to find a good Christian girl like you on her knees beside the bed."

"Well, all right," blushed the bride, "but that way it always gives me hiccups."

Just people are such... Their minds are conditioned in such a way. The poor preacher is thinking of prayer, but the girl is thinking of something else.

Henry Ford died, and before going to heaven was interviewed by God. Asked about his achievements on the earth, Henry Ford boasted, "My model-T Ford is one of the greatest achievements of all time. Incidentally, what do you think about it?"

God smiled and said, "It was not a bad invention." And he asked Henry what he thought about his greatest creation—woman.

"Not bad," said Henry. "But if you ask me, the inlet valve is a bit too near the exhaust."

A Henry Ford is a Henry Ford; he understands only one language. Your old mind understands only one thing: how to protect yourself. But life belongs to those who drop all defense measures, because every defense measure is a mistrust in existence.

Life belongs to those who trust existence. Then there is no need for any defense. Then this is your home...all these stars and all these oceans and all these mountains are part of your home. This whole existence is your very life's source. There is no need to fear, and there is no need to close yourself in dark cells in a deep mistrust.

Mistrust is almost death.

Trust is the only life that I know of.

Okay Maneesha?

Yes, Osho.

7

BEWARE OF THE MIND: IT IS BLIND

I will not tell you to make an effort to understand the roots of your mind and its patterns; it is simply a useless wastage of time. Just awareness is enough, more than enough. As you become aware, you come out of the grip of the mind, and the mind remains almost a dead fossil.

Beloved Osho,

Do I have to know and understand the roots of my old patterns in order to be able to drop them, or is awareness enough? Please comment.

Deva Suparni, this is the dividing line between Western psychology and Eastern mysticism. Western psychology is an effort to understand the roots of your old patterns, but it does not help anybody to get rid of them.

You become more understanding, you become more sober, you become more normal; your mind is no longer a great mess. Things are settled a little better than they ever have been before, but every problem remains the same—it simply goes dormant. You can understand your jealousy, you can understand your anger, your hate, your greed, your ambitions, but all this understanding will remain intellectual. So even the greatest psychologists of the West are far away from the Eastern mystics.

The man who founded Western psychology, Sigmund Freud, was so much afraid of death that even the mention of the word 'death' was enough to throw him into a coma; he would become unconscious, the paranoia of death was so great. It happened three times. He was so much afraid of ghosts that he would not pass by the side of a cemetery. Now, a man like Sigmund Freud who has tremendous intellectual acumen, who knows every root of the mind, who knows every subtle functioning of the mind, still remains confined in the mind.

Awareness leads you beyond the mind. It does not bother to understand the problems of the mind, their roots, it simply leaves the mind aside, it simply gets out of it. That is the reason why in the East there has been no development of psychology.

It is strange that for ten thousand years at least, the East has been consistently and one-pointedly working in the field of human consciousness, but it has not developed any psychology, any psychoanalysis or psychosynthesis. It is a great surprise that for ten thousand years nobody even touched the matter. Rather than understanding the mind, the East developed a totally different approach, and their approach was disidentifying with the mind: "I am not the mind." Once this awareness becomes crystallized in you, the mind becomes impotent.

The whole power of the mind is in your identification with it. So it was found to be useless to go unnecessarily digging for roots, finding causes behind causes, working out through dreams, analyzing dreams, interpreting dreams. And every psychologist finds a different root, finds a different interpretation, finds a different cause. Psychology is not yet a science; it is still fictitious.

If you go to Sigmund Freud, your dream will be interpreted in sexual terms. His mind is obsessed with sex. Bring anything and immediately he will find an interpretation that it is sexual.

Go to Alfred Adler, the man who founded another school of psychology—analytical psychology... He is obsessed with another idea: will to power. So whatever you dream will be interpreted according to that idea—it is will to power. Go to Carl Gustav Jung, he interprets every dream as a faraway echo from your past lives. His interpretation is mythological. And there are many other schools.

There has been a great effort made by Assagioli—psychosynthesis—to bring all these schools together, but his psychosynthesis is absolutely useless. At least psychoanalysis has some truth in it, and analytical psychology also has some truth in it; but psychosynthesis is simply a hodge-podge. It has taken one part from one school, another part from another school, and it has joined them together.

Assagioli is a great intellectual; he could manage to put the pieces of the jigsaw puzzle in the right places. But what was significant in Sigmund Freud was significant in a certain context; that context is no longer there. He has only taken what appears to be significant, but without the context it loses all meaning. Hence, Assagioli has worked his whole life for some synthesis, but he has not been able to create anything significant. And all these schools have been working hard.

But the East simply bypassed the mind. Rather than finding out the causes and roots and reasons, they found out one thing: from where does the mind get its power? from where does the energy come to feed it? The energy to feed the mind comes from your identification that "I am it." They broke that bridge. That's what awareness is: being aware that "I am not the body, I am not the mind. I am not even the heart, I am simply pure awareness, a *sakshi*."

As this awareness deepens, becomes crystallized, the mind has more and more a shadow existence. Its impact on you loses all force. And when the awareness is a hundred percent settled, mind simply evaporates.

Western psychology has still to figure out why it is not succeeding. Thousands of people are going through psychoanalysis and through other therapeutic methods, but not a single one of them—not even the founder of those schools—can be called enlightened, can be said to be without problems, can be said to be without anxieties, anguishes, fears, paranoia. Everything exists in them as it exists in you.

Sigmund Freud was asked many times by his disciples, "You psychoanalyze all of us; we bring our dreams to you to be interpreted. It will be a great experiment if you allow us to psychoanalyze you. You give us your dreams and we will try to analyze and find out what they mean, from where they come, what they indicate." But Sigmund Freud never agreed to that. That shows an immense weakness in the whole framework of psychoanalysis. He was afraid that they would find the same things in his dreams that he was finding in their dreams. Then his superiority as a founder, as a master would be lost.

He was not aware at all of people like Gautam Buddha or Mahavira or Nagarjuna. Because these people don't dream, there is nothing to analyze. These people have come so far away from the mind that all connections are cut. They live out of awareness, not out of intellect. They respond out of awareness, not out of mind and its memories. And they don't repress anything; hence there is no need for any dreaming.

Dreaming is a by-product of repression. There are aboriginal tribes where people don't dream. Or if they dream, they dream only once in a while. They are surprised to know that civilized people dream almost the whole night. In eight hours' sleep, six hours you are dreaming. And the aboriginal is simply sleeping eight hours in deep silence, with no disturbance. Sigmund Freud was aware only of the sick Western people. He was not aware of a man of awareness; otherwise the whole history of Western psychology would have been different.

I will not tell you, Suparni, to make an effort to understand the roots of your mind and its patterns; it is simply a useless wastage of time. Just awareness is enough, more than enough. As you become aware, you come out of the grip of the mind, and the mind remains almost a dead fossil. There is no need to bother from where the greed came, the real question is how to get out of it. The question is not from where the ego arose—these are intellectual questions which are not significant for a seeker.

And then there will be many philosophical standpoints: from where greed arose, from where ego came in; from where your jealousy, from where your hate, from where your cruelty came in—looking for the beginnings of all this. And mind is a vast complex; in fact, life is too small to figure out all the problems of the mind and their origins. Their origins may be of thousands of lives. Slowly Western psychology is coming closer to it—for example, primal therapy.

Janov understood that unless we find the beginnings of the problems... That means to him, being a Christian, believing only in one life—the roots must be found somewhere in childhood. So he started working to remind you of your childhood, and then he stumbled upon a new fact—that in deep hypnosis people not only remember their childhood, they remember their birth. They also remember the nine months in the mother's womb, and a few very sensitive people even remember their previous life.

And then he became afraid himself, that he was going into a tunnel which seemed to be unending. You go into the past life and that will take you again, through the whole long passage, to another life. Your mind is many lives old, so you are not going to be able to find its root in the present. Perhaps you will have to travel backwards through thousands of lives, and it is not an easy thing. And then too, even if you come to understand from where the greed has come, it does not make any change. You will have to then know how to drop it.

And there are so many problems that if you start dropping each problem separately, you will need millions of lives to be completely finished with the mind. And while you are figuring out about one problem, other problems are growing, gathering more energy, more vitality, more influence. It is a very stupid game.

In the East, not a single person in the whole past—in China, in India, in Japan, in Arabia—has ever bothered about it. It is fighting with shadows. They worked from a very different angle and they succeeded immensely. They simply pulled their awareness out of the mind. They stood outside the mind as a witness and they found a miracle happening: as they became a witness, the mind became impotent, it lost all power over them. And there was no need to understand anything.

Awareness goes on growing higher and the mind goes on growing smaller—in the same proportion. If awareness is fifty percent then mind is cut to fifty percent. If awareness is seventy percent, only thirty percent of the mind remains. The day awareness is a hundred percent, there is no mind to be found at all.

Hence, the whole Eastern approach is to find a state of no-mind—that silence, that purity, that serenity. And mind is no longer there with all its problems, with all its roots; it has simply evaporated the way dewdrops evaporate in the sun in the morning, leaving no trace behind. Hence I will say to you, awareness is not only enough, it is more than enough. You don't need anything else.

Western psychology has no place for meditation in it yet, and that's why it goes on going round and round, finding no solution. There are people who have been in psychoanalysis for fifteen years. They have wasted fortunes on it—because psychoanalysis is the most highly paid profession. Fifteen years in psychoanalysis and all that has happened is that they have become addicted to psychoanalysis. Now they cannot remain without it. Rather than solving any problem, a new problem has arisen. Now it has become almost like a drug addiction. So when they get fed up with one psychoanalyst, they start with another. If they are not being psychoanalyzed, then they feel something is missing.

But it has not helped anybody. Even they accept that there is not a single man in the whole West who has been completely analyzed. But such is the blindness of people that they cannot see the simple point, why a single person is not there—when there are thousands of psychoanalysts analyzing people—who has been perfectly analyzed and who has gone beyond mind.

Analysis cannot take you beyond. The way beyond is awareness, the way beyond mind is meditation. It is a simple way and it has created thousands of enlightened people in the East. And they were not doing anything with the mind, they were doing something else: they were simply becoming aware, alert, conscious. They were using mind also as an object.

The way you see a tree, the way you see pillars, the way you see other people—they were trying to see the mind also as separate, and they succeeded. And the moment they succeeded in seeing the mind as separate, that was the death of the mind. In its place grows a clarity; intellect disappears, intelligence arises. One does not react anymore, one responds. Reaction is always based on your past experiences, and response is just like a mirror: you come in front of it and it responds, it shows your face. It does not carry any memory. The moment you have moved away, it is again pure, no reflection.

The meditator becomes finally a mirror. Any situation is reflected in him and he responds in the present moment, out of presence. Hence, his every response has a newness, a freshness, a clarity, a beauty, a grace. It is not some old idea that he is repeating. This is something to be understood, that no situation is ever exactly the same as any other situation that you have encountered before. So if you are reacting out of the past, you are not able to tackle the situation; you are lagging far behind.

That is the cause of your failure. You don't see the situation, you are more concerned with your response; you are blind to the situation. The man of meditation is simply open with his eyes, available to see the situation and let the situation provoke the response in him. He is not carrying a ready-made answer to it.

A beautiful story about Gautam Buddha.... One morning a man asked him, "Is there a God?" Buddha looked at the man, looked into his eyes and said, "No, there is no God."

That very day in the afternoon another man asked, "What do you think about God? Is there a God?" Again he looked at the man and into his eyes and said, "Yes, there is a God."

Ananda, who was with him, became very much puzzled, but he was always very careful not to interfere in anything. He had his time when everybody had left in the night and Buddha was going to sleep; if he had to ask anything, he would ask at that time.

But by the evening, as the sun was setting, a third man came with almost the same question, formulated differently. He said, "There are people who believe in God, there are people who don't believe in God. I myself don't know with whom I should stand. You help me."

Ananda was very intensely listening now to what Buddha says. He had given two absolutely contradictory answers in the same day, and now the third opportunity has arisen—and there is no third answer. But Buddha gave him the third answer. He did not speak, he closed his eyes. It was a beautiful evening. The birds had settled in their trees—Buddha was staying in a mango grove—the sun had set, a cool breeze had started blowing. The man, seeing Buddha sitting with closed eyes, thought that perhaps this is his answer, so he also sat with closed eyes with him.

An hour passed, the man opened his eyes, touched the feet of Buddha and said, "Your compassion is great. You have given me the answer. I will always remain obliged to you."

Ananda could not believe it, because Buddha had not spoken a single word. And as the man went away, perfectly satisfied and contented, Ananda asked Buddha, "This is too much! You should think of me—you will drive me mad. I am just on the verge of a nervous breakdown. To one man you say there is no God, to another man you say there is a God, and to the third you don't answer. And that strange fellow says that he has received the answer and he is perfectly satisfied and obliged, and touches your feet. What is going on?"

Buddha said, "Ananda, the first thing you have to remember is, those were not your questions, those answers were not given to you. Why did you get unnecessarily concerned with other people's problems? First solve your own problems."

Ananda said, "That's true, they were not my questions and the answers were not given to me. But what can I do? I have ears and I hear, and I have heard and I have seen, and now my whole being is puzzled—what is right?"

Buddha said, "Right? Right is awareness. The first man was a theist. He wanted my support—he already believed in God. He had come with an answer, ready-made, just to solicit my support so that he can go around and say, 'I am right, even Buddha thinks so.' I had to say no to him, just to disturb his belief, because belief is not knowing. The second man was an atheist. He had also come with a ready-made answer, that there is no God, and he wanted my support to strengthen his disbelief and so he can go on proclaiming around that I agree with him. I had to say to him, 'Yes, God exists.' But my purpose was the same.

"If you see my purpose, there is no contradiction. I was disturbing the first man's preconceived belief, I was disturbing the second person's preconceived disbelief. Belief is positive, disbelief is negative, but both are the same. Neither of them was a knower and neither of them was a humble seeker; they were already carrying a prejudice.

"The third man was a seeker. He had no prejudice, he had opened his heart. He told me, 'There are people who believe, there are people who don't believe. I myself don't know whether God exists or not. Help me.' And the only help I could give was to teach him a lesson of silent awareness; words were useless. And as I closed my eyes he understood the hint. He was a man of certain intelligence—open, vulnerable. He closed his eyes.

"As I moved deeper into silence, as he became part of the field of my silence and my presence, he started moving into silence, moving into awareness. When one hour had passed, it seemed as if only a few minutes had passed. He had not received any answer in words, but he had received the authentic answer in silence: don't be bothered about God; it does not matter whether God exists or does not exist. What matters is whether silence exists, awareness exists or not. If you are silent and aware, you yourself are a god. God is not something far away from you; either you are a mind or you are a god. In silence and awareness mind melts and disappears and reveals your divineness to you. Although I have not said anything to him, he has received the answer, and received it in a perfectly right way."

Awareness brings you to a point where you are able to see with your own eyes the ultimate reality of yourself and the universe...and a miraculous experience that you and the universe are not separate, that you are part of the whole. To me this is the only meaning of holy.

You have been trained for analysis, for understanding, for intellectual gymnastics. Those things are not going to help anybody; they have never helped anybody. That's why the West lacks one most precious dimension—that of enlightenment, awakening. All its richness is nothing in comparison to the richness that comes from enlightenment, from achieving the state of no-mind.

So don't get entangled with the mind; rather become a watcher by the side of the road and let the mind pass on the road. Soon the road will be empty. The mind lives as a parasite. You are identified with it; that is its life. Your awareness cuts the connection, it becomes its death.

The ancient scriptures of the East say that the master is a death—a very strange statement, but of immense meaning. The master is a death because meditation is the death of the mind, meditation is the death of the ego. Meditation is the death of your personality and the birth and the resurrection of your essential being. And to know that essential being is to know all.

Becky Goldberg phoned down to the hotel manager. "I am up here in room five hundred and ten," she shouted angrily, "and I want you to know there is a man walking around the room across the way stark naked, and his blinds are up."

"I will be up right away," said the manager. He entered Becky's room, peered through the window and said, "You are right Madam, the man does appear to be naked. But his window still covers him from the waist down, no matter where he is in the room."

"Ah, yes," yelled Becky. "Just stand on the bed, just stand on the bed!"

Mind is a strange fellow. Where there is no problem, it creates a problem. Why should you stand on the bed? Just to find that somebody is naked in his room? One has to be aware of all these stupidities of the mind. I don't agree with the theory of evolution of Charles Darwin, but I have a certain respect for the theory, because it may not be historically true that the monkeys became men, but it is certainly psychologically true—because man's mind is just like a monkey...stupid in every way.

There is no point in digging deep into the rubbish of the mind. It is not your being, it is not you; it is just the dust that you have gathered through many, many lives around you.

A young woman went to the doctor, afraid that she had gangrene because of two small spots, one on each of her thighs. The doctor examined her carefully and then told her it was not gangrene and she had nothing to worry about. "But by the way," he asked the girl as she was leaving, "is your boyfriend a gypsy?"

"Yes," replied the girl, "as a matter of fact he is."

"Well," said the doctor, "tell him that his earrings are not gold."

These are mind's functionings.

It is a great discoverer.

The old definition of a philosopher is that he is blind in a dark night, in a dark house where there is no light, and he is searching for a black cat which is not there. But this is not all: he finds her! And he writes great treatises, theses, systems, proves logically the existence of the black cat.

Beware of the mind: it is blind. It has never known anything but it is a great pretender. It pretends to know everything.

Socrates has categorized humanity into two classes. One class he calls the knowledgeably ignorant: the people who think they know and they are basically ignorant; that is the work of the mind. And the second category he calls the ignorant knowers: the people who think, "We don't know." In their humbleness, in their innocence, descends knowing.

So there are pretenders of knowledge—that is the function of the mind—and there are humble people who say, "We don't know." In their innocence there is knowledge, and that is the work of meditation and awareness.

Beloved Osho,

At the end of the meditations I sometimes reach a quiet, expanding space inside me. It is like a feeling of vastness and it relaxes me very much. Then, after some time I get tense and afraid and the vastness reaches a barrier and disappears. Each time, the silence during this experience has something unbearable in it. Beloved Osho, what is the barrier that I encounter?

Anand Nirbija, the question that you have asked is significant for all meditators. The first experience of silence is heavy for the simple reason that it is the entry into the unknown. You are well accustomed to the known, familiar. With the unknown, entering into a space without boundaries, you are absolutely unfamiliar, and the same fear arises in you as the fear that arises in a dewdrop which is slipping from the lotus leaf into the ocean. It is a kind of death; it will never be again a dewdrop. It is losing itself into the vastness of the ocean. But it is only in the beginning. Soon the realization turns into a totally different experience.

When it happened to one of the mystics, one of the greatest mystics, Kabir, he wrote a small, beautiful poem, which means: I had gone in search for truth; truth is found but I am no more. There was the seeker—then the sought was not there. Now the sought is there but the seeker is no more. My dewdrop existence has fallen into the ocean, and now there is no way to take it out.

Before dying, he told his son, Kamal, "Just write another statement. The first line remains the same: I had gone to seek the truth; the truth is found but the seeker is lost. But change the second line: I was a dewdrop. Now the whole ocean has fallen into me and there is no way to be separated from the ocean."

In the beginning you will feel you are getting lost. In the end you will find that that which was false is lost and you have gained immense territory...the infinite silence, unbounded bliss. You are no longer there as you used to be. You are no longer a mind, you are just a pure awareness. Hence, the first experience becomes unbearable. One trembles—the fear of getting lost... One clings to the lotus leaf. The vast ocean creates a great danger—danger to your personality, danger to you as you have known yourself up to now. But it is just in the beginning.

One of the very significant statements of Gautam the Buddha is, "That which is sweet in the beginning, beware of it, because in the end it will turn into bitterness. And that which is bitter in the beginning...have courage, it will turn into sweetness in the end." That bitterness in the beginning is your test, whether you are worthy to have that sweetness that is waiting for you in the end.

I will read your question: "At the end of the meditations I sometimes reach a quiet, expanding space inside me. It is like a feeling of vastness and relaxes me very much. Then, after some time I get tense and afraid and the vastness reaches a barrier and disappears. Each time, the silence during this experience has something unbearable in it. What is the barrier that I encounter?"

It is good news. Everyone who goes from the mundane to the sacred comes to a barrier. Finally he understands it is not a barrier but a bridge, but that is when he has passed it. From this side it looks like a barrier. Once you have passed to the other side you are surprised that it was a bridge, but it was so unknown that you could not have understood it as a bridge.

You have known barriers in your life; you have never known bridges. Hence, you interpreted it according to your experience. Next time, when you encounter that barrier, pass through it as if it is a bridge. Of course it will be only "as if" for you, but once you have passed it, that "as if" will drop. You will have a good laughter at yourself. And silence seems to be unbearable because you are so accustomed to noise.

Aldous Huxley, one of the most intelligent people of this age, wanted to experience silence—Western style. So he went into a scientific lab where they had an absolutely soundproof room for their own experiments. Those experiments were going on at that time for the astronauts, because of all the problems that a man who is going to the moon is going to face after he leaves the two hundred miles of air around the earth, the greatest problem is the silence, deafening silence. So they were training the travelers in space for all those experiences that they may encounter and may find very difficult—but if they know something of it, it will be easier for them. That absolutely soundproof room was created for that purpose.

Aldous Huxley remembers that when he entered the room he could not believe that silence can be so heavy. He became so afraid, knowing perfectly well that he is in a room which is soundproof, no noise can enter it. But his ears, his body, everything was accustomed to vibrations all around. You are

sitting here, you are listening to a few noises: the birds in the trees,
I am speaking to you...and there are many sounds which you are
not listening to but your body feels the vibes.

All the radio waves are passing through you. You can catch
any radio station with just a small transistor set. Do you think that
transistor set creates those waves? Those waves are passing; the
transistor set is simply capable of catching them. They are
touching your body. You are surrounded by millions of radio
waves which you are not hearing, but you are accustomed to them.
That has been your whole life's experience.

Aldous Huxley felt a few things: one, as if he was naked—and
he was wearing his clothes! What happened? Why was he feeling
naked? All those subtle clothes of vibrations that are surrounding
you were no longer there. And his ears started hurting...strange!
One can feel one's ears hurting when somebody is shouting or
some great noise is there. But because there was no noise, the ears
came into an absolutely unknown territory. It was unbelievable.

He had asked to remain there for one hour, but he remained
only for five minutes, and he started knocking: "Open the door. It
is too much! It feels...I may burst, I may fall apart"—because the
support of all the waves around you is keeping you together.

When you go into deep silence within you, it is also a very
strange experience in the beginning. It creates fear—inside your
silence you know that the identity you had of yourself is
absolutely false. Your name is false, your form is false, your body
is just a separate thing from you, and you don't find anything solid
inside to cling to. In fact, you find you are the silence...a kind of
nothingness, nobodiness.

Gautam Buddha has the right words for this experience. One
is *anatta*; you feel a state of no-selfness. The second is *shunyata*;
you find yourself just a zero. And the third is that there is no hint
of any "I." The silence is so deafening—and you are it—that one
feels like running out into the well-known world, howsoever
miserable, howsoever full of suffering. But anyway we are
accustomed to it.

The astronauts have gone through strange experiences, which
mystics have always gone through—Eastern style—just by going

inside. As the rocket leaves the gravitation sphere of the earth, for the first time you don't have any weight and it is such a shock. You start floating in the spacecraft. Unless you keep your belt on, you cannot remain in your seat. You are just floating, touching the top, and everything else that is loose is also floating. Because there is no longer any gravitation, you don't have any weight.

Albert Einstein had an idea which most probably will be found to be accurate, because he was the man who worked the hardest as far as space travel is concerned. His idea is mind boggling. He himself kept it for many months and did not announce it to the scientific world because he was afraid that nobody was going to believe him. The idea was such that people would think he had gone cuckoo. But the idea was so significant that he finally decided that he could risk his sanity but he had to declare it.

The idea was that beyond gravitation you stop aging. If a man leaves the earth for a faraway star, and if it takes thirty years for him to reach that star and then coming back again another thirty years, and when he had left the earth he was thirty years old, then if you think that by the time he comes back he will be ninety years old, you are wrong. He will still be thirty years old. All his friends and colleagues may be already in their graves. Perhaps one or two may still be with one foot in the grave, one foot out. But he will be as young as when he had left.

The moment you are out of gravitation, the aging process stops. Aging is continuously a certain burden on your body. The earth goes on pulling you and you are fighting the pull. Your energy is disturbed and destroyed in this continuous fight. But when you are out of the gravitational field of the earth you simply remain as you were. You will not find your contemporaries; you will not find all those fashions that were current when you left. You will find that sixty years have passed.

But the feeling of going beyond gravitation can happen even in meditation—it happens. And that has misled many people. With your closed eyes, when you are absolutely silent you are out of gravitation. But just your silence is out of gravitation, not your body. But in that moment you are identified with your silence, so you feel as if you are moving upwards; that is called by yoga "levitation."

And without opening your eyes you will feel not only that it is a feeling, but that your body is actually moving upwards. But that is only a fallacy. Your silence is beyond gravitation—that is a true experience. But because you are identified still with the body, you feel as if your body is moving. If you open your eyes you will find yourself sitting in the same posture on the ground.

Just now there is a case in the Supreme Court of America against Maharishi Mahesh Yogi by seven disciples, asking him for ninety million dollars for deceiving them—because he promised that they would be able to levitate with their body and that did not happen. Whenever they opened their eyes they were sitting on the ground, although when their eyes were closed they felt that it was happening.

Maharishi Mahesh Yogi has been charging people for teaching them levitation, but he has not been able even to give one public demonstration. It is exploitation in the name of spirituality. Certainly those people feel it, but they should keep their eyes closed. If they open their eyes everything is disturbed, they are sitting on the ground. If you continue for hours the feeling of going up, going up, you can move beyond the house, you can move beyond the trees, you can move beyond the mountains—but don't open your eyes because you are sitting where you are sitting.

It is just the experience of your silence; your silence is moving beyond gravitation. And I don't think Maharishi Mahesh Yogi is going to prove anything in the Supreme Court. He has been asked again and again to give a public demonstration, but no public demonstration is possible. It is an old, known fact that meditators have always felt themselves going up, but that is purely a spiritual experience, nothing physical. What he has done is try to make it appear as if it is physical, and thousands of people have paid him two hundred and fifty dollars for the training.

It is very easy to exploit people in the name of spirituality and to give them a sense that they have not been exploited. The only condition is, keep your eyes closed and you will feel it, and you will go home with the feeling that you have attained levitation.

It is possible for you also to have that experience—don't be afraid, you are not going anywhere; you are sitting perfectly in your place. But all these experiences can create fear. Knowing it well that they create fear—but the fear is unfounded—one needs just a little courage to get accustomed to the unknown and the fear disappears.

A new group of husbands had just arrived in heaven. The welcoming angel looked them over and said, "Okay, all you men who were henpecked on the earth please step to the left. All those who were the boss of the house please step to the right."

The line quickly formed on the left. Only one man, Hymie Goldberg, stepped to the right. Seeing Hymie looking more like a mouse than a lion, the angel inquired, "And what makes you think that you belong on the right side?"

"Well," squeaked Hymie, "this is where my wife told me to stand."

A lifelong habit of listening to the wife...even though he is dead, now there is no wife around. The gap is unbridgeable—the wife is in the world and he is in heaven—but the old habit... The wife has even instructed him: "Don't stand in a crowd." And on the left certainly everybody was standing, so naturally he had to stand on the right.

Habits die hard, and we have so many mundane habits that when you enter into the world of the sacred you will feel you are being robbed of everything. But remember, whatever you are robbed of was false. Don't cling to it; that will become the barrier—let it go. Whatever is yours will always be yours, there is no way to rob you of it.

A man was in a Turkish bath when he looked up and saw someone stealing his clothes. He took off after the man, covering his private parts with his hat. As he turned the corner, he bumped straight into two girls who looked at him and burst out laughing. "If you were ladies," he shouted, "you would not laugh at a man in my circumstances!"

"And if you were a gentleman," replied one of the girls, "you would raise your hat."

This is our known world—ladies and gentlemen. When you enter into the unknown you are neither a man nor a woman, you are neither a mind nor a heart; you are something that can only be called "X." It is better not to give any name to it, because any name will come from your vocabulary of the known. Let it remain unknown, mysterious; just don't be worried, don't be afraid.

And I say this not because it is written in some scriptures, I say this because I have passed through the same problems, the same fear, the same desire to turn back, the same barrier which proved finally to be a bridge. So whatever I am saying to you, I am saying with the absolute authority of my own experience. I am not saying to believe me, I am saying just to experiment. Let my words be just hypothetical—perhaps your experiment will prove whether they are true or untrue—don't believe in them beforehand, remain open.

I can allow you to remain open; no religion leaves you open. They say, "Believe." And the reason is that the people who had experienced may have died twenty centuries before, and now the people who are representing them have no experience of their own. They are afraid that if you don't believe...they themselves are not certain what they are saying, whether it is true or not. They believe; hence they insist that you believe.

I don't believe, I know. Hence, I insist: experiment without any belief and you will know.

Once somebody asked Raman Maharishi, "Do you believe in God?" and he said, "No." The man was shocked; he had come from far away, hearing that Raman Maharishi was an enlightened being. He thought perhaps he had been misunderstood, or he had misunderstood. He repeated his question. Raman Maharishi said, "I have heard it rightly, you have heard it rightly; there is no need to repeat it. I don't believe in God because I know."

Belief is for those who do not know. My effort with you is not to give you belief systems, but to give you hypothetical ideas to experiment on. And I have a certainty that you will come to the same conclusions. There is no other possibility.

Okay, Maneesha?

Yes, Osho.

8

JOURNALISM: MAKING SAINTS OUT OF CRIMINALS

Journalists can do a tremendous service to humanity if their minds are clear, if they are not themselves prejudiced, either in favor of spiritualism or in favor of materialism. A journalist has to be of an open mind, receptive to all kinds of possibilities. He has to be a seeker and a searcher and an agnostic; he has not to be a believer.

Beloved Osho,

You are the greatest marketing person of a product that gratifies the soul. We are in the business of selling a product that gratifies the mind; there are others who sell products that gratify the body. What lessons can we learn from You to effectively market mind and body products?

Sameer, I am reminded by your question of an anecdote. H.G. Wells had completed his great work on the history of the world.... And he has made tremendously important statements in his rare book. For example, he has said about Gautam Buddha that "He was the most godless, yet the most godly man that has ever walked on the earth."

His book was the talk of all the intellectuals around the world, and one intellectual journalist interviewed him about the book. His first question was, "What do you think about civilization?" And the answer that H.G. Wells gave is of such depth that it has not to be forgotten; it is still fresh and new. He said, "The idea of civilization is good, but somebody must do something about it, because it is still an idea. Civilization has not happened. Researching for my book on world history, I have come to know that man is still uncivilized."

And one of the reasons man is still uncivilized is the division between mind, body, and soul. This division has been preached by all the religions of the world. They have condemned the body; a few of them have condemned the mind, too. And they have all praised the soul. The result has not been as they expected. The result has been a very strange poisoning of humanity. People have not dropped their bodies, they have not dropped their minds, but they have become guilty about them. They have lost self-respect, they have lost touch with the wisdom of their own bodies, and they have lost the mastery of their own minds. And the reality is that unless all three function in a total organic unity, a man is not whole.

One who is not whole is not holy either.

My basic approach is: I am not against the body, I am not against the mind; I am all for a unity, a symphony, a synchronicity amongst these three spheres. And a man will be fulfilled only, complete only, when all three are functioning in total harmony.

In the East, the body has been so much condemned that the ultimate result is poverty—no science, no technology, a poor, hungry body; starved, condemned, neglected. And in the West, the result has been a healthy body, an evolved technology, richer literature, art, all for the nourishment of the mind, but a poor soul, almost nonexistential. This is a strange tragedy. The West is suffering from a poor soul, and the East is suffering from a poor body and a poor mind.

My suggestion to you, Sameer, is that the work for the future humanity, for a new man, is to drop the old conditioning—of the East, and of the West. Drop all antagonism, either of the spiritualist or of the materialist. Accept the realistic approach that existence is both—matter on the outside and spirit on the inside. And in between the two is the bridge of the mind.

In a miniature form, the same is true about every human being. The new man will come out of this unity.

It feels...if somebody says that Gautam Buddha is only half, it hurts. But truth is truth. Mahavira is half—just a soul, anti-life. So is Zorba—against spirituality. So are all the scientists—even the greatest, like Albert Einstein—who cannot conceive the possibility that there is an interior existence of consciousness.

Albert Einstein is half; that is the tragedy of the West. Buddha is half; that is our tragedy. And the work for the future is to bring them together.

I have been using one expression, and that is "Zorba the Buddha." The body has to be enjoyed as much as your soul. Matter has its own beauty, its own power, just as consciousness has its own world, its own silence, its own peace, its own ecstasy. And between the two is the area of the mind—something of matter and something of the spirit. The poet is just in the middle, between the materialist and the spiritualist; his poetry touches both extremes. I would like all three points—the two extremes and the middle—to become one unity.

A man who rejoices in his body and the wisdom of the body, a man who uses his mind as a tremendously significant mechanism that evolution has brought, and a man who does not stop at mind but goes on searching beyond, into the realms of divineness, into the realms of godliness—to produce this man should be the effort of all those who are in some way concerned with educating the new generation. The educationists, the journalists, the spiritual teachers—all people who are involved in some way in creating a better human being than has been possible in the past—have to accept the totality of man without rejecting anything.

Journalists can do a tremendous service to humanity if their minds are clear, if they are not themselves prejudiced, either in favor of spiritualism or in favor of materialism. A journalist has to be of an open mind, receptive to all kinds of possibilities. He has to be a seeker and a searcher and an agnostic; he has not to be a believer. The moment you believe in something, you start enforcing your belief, whether it is right or wrong. The journalist has to be open to all dimensions, ready to accept anything that is going to beautify existence and make man more blissful, more healthy, more intelligent, more aware of the tremendous mystery that surrounds us.

To me, that is the only prayer: to become aware of the miraculous, the mysterious that surrounds us. And only a man who has come to a unity within himself is capable of understanding the mystery of existence.

Beloved Osho,

When a person enters a temple, one feels a sense of sensory appeasement—music, chanting, incense, prasad, the visual beauty of the architecture, etc. Can corporate houses, the temples of the modern age, have anything to learn from this?

Sameer, not only the corporate houses but every place where man dwells has much to learn from the temples. First, you are always moving on holy ground. Not only in the temple are you in a holy place, but even in the marketplace you are moving on the same holy ground. You are not to be just prayerful in the temple, in the mosque, in the church. Your prayerfulness has to become just your breathing. You have not to create only in your temple a beautiful world of incense, of flowers, of music, of chanting, of beautiful architecture, of sculptures—the temple should simply be the model for every house. Not only corporate houses, every house should be a temple, because every body is a temple.

God dwells in you, and wherever you are, you should create the aroma, the fragrance of godliness.

The authentically religious person is neither Hindu, nor Mohammedan, nor Christian, nor Jaina, nor Buddhist. An authentic religious person is simply a prayerful person, a loving person, a creative person—a man who has the golden touch; whatever he touches becomes beautiful and valuable.

It is not possible that our houses remain in hell and once in a while, for an hour, we can enter a temple and find heaven—that is not possible. Unless you are twenty-four hours in heaven, you cannot enter into a temple and suddenly change—suddenly drop your jealousies, your anger, your hatred, your competitiveness, your ambitions, your politics. You cannot simply drop all your ugliness.

You can pretend, you can be a hypocrite ...and in fact all the people who are visiting temples of any religion are hypocrites, because their other twenty-three hours show their reality. For only one hour, they cannot become a different being.

A religious person has to understand that it is not a question of believing in a certain theology; it is not a question of believing in a certain tradition. It is a question of transforming yourself in such a way that compassion becomes your very heartbeat, that gratitude becomes your very breathing, that wherever you are, your eyes can see the divine—in the trees, in the mountains, in people, in animals, in birds. Unless you can make the whole existence your temple, you are not religious.

Wherever you move, you are always in a temple, because you are always surrounded by that mysterious energy that people have called "God." A few others have given it other names—they differ only in names. But one thing is certain: we are not living in a mundane universe. On each step there is a mystery, and there are mysteries beyond mysteries. If you are simply aware of all the mysteries, your worship will be to make everything as worthy of God as possible.

Sitting in your shop, you should be waiting for a customer who is going to be a god....

Kabir became enlightened, and even kings were his disciples. They all said to him, "Now it is time: you stop weaving clothes. It hurts our pride. People laugh at us, they say, 'Your master has to function like a poor weaver. The whole week he weaves clothes and then he takes the clothes on his own shoulders to the marketplace. It does not look right for a man who has so many disciples. Can't you take care of him?'"

But Kabir insisted, "It is not a question of my livelihood, it is a question that some god will be coming to the market to purchase what I have woven with such love, with such gratitude, with such meditativeness. And if he does not find me there...I cannot do that.

As long as I am alive, I will go on serving God by the only art that I know—that is weaving."

And he made clothes with such love, with such prayerfulness, with such grace, that you could feel that this man is not only weaving clothes—he is weaving something more; something spiritual is being woven into the clothes. And in the market every customer was addressed by Kabir as "Ram," the Indian word for God. "Ram, I have been waiting so long for you; where have you gone? It is time for the closing of the market, the sun is setting, and I am waiting for you."

And at first customers used to be very puzzled: this great saint calls them 'Ram'? By and by they became accustomed to the fact, and they started behaving in a different way—it was not a question of being a shopkeeper and a customer, it was a question of being two lovers. It was a love affair.

I would like all corporate houses to be temples—but not only corporate houses; I would like every house, every kitchen, every bedroom, to be a temple. And I would like you to behave with everybody.... He may be your enemy, but still he has deep in his being the same source of life you have. You have to be respectful to his being, as much as you are respectful to your friend. Your wife should be as much respected as any goddess in any temple.

I cannot believe that people who have been pretending up to now to be religious, have behaved with women in such a barbarous way, and they have not seen any shadow of God in the woman. The same religious people have behaved with the poorest of the poor—the *sudras*, the untouchables—as inhuman beings. They could not see. They could see gods in stone statues, but they could not see in living beings that a god is throbbing in their hearts just as he is throbbing within you.

I want to say it with absolute certainty: these people were not religious. Just as civilization has not happened yet, religion also has not happened yet. We have to create the space where religion, civilization, culture, can happen. They are different aspects of the same consciousness, of the same awareness.

Beloved Osho,

For a commercial organization, marketing is the ultimate life source; however, some marketing professionals suffer from an element of contradiction in their personal lives. Vis-a-vis professional objectives, are we selling things to people that they don't need?

Sameer, the question is a little complex—complex because in a way you are selling people what they need...but whether their need is sick or healthy is a totally different matter.

You are fulfilling people's sick needs. And that should be felt as a responsibility. Needs have to be fulfilled, but you have to learn a great discrimination: what are the sick needs, and what are the healthy needs?

For example, pornography is a need. And millions of people are providing pornographic literature, photography, all kinds of pornographic films, blue films. They certainly are fulfilling a need—people have been so repressed sexually for centuries that they are hungry to see the naked woman. Certainly your business prospers, but you are depending on a very ugly exploitation of people.

The responsibility of the journalist is great: he has to make people aware—why do they need pornography? In an aboriginal tribe, nobody is interested in pornographic literature because people are almost naked; they don't have any clothes. From the very childhood, the boys and the girls become aware of each other's bodies, it is a natural acquaintance. They never become peeping Toms. And they will not be interested in magazines like Playboy. But in our so-called civilized society, people are hiding Playboys in the *Shrimad Bhagavadgita*, in the *Holy Bible*, because that is the safest place to hide anything; nobody opens it. Who bothers to look into the *Holy Bible*, or the *Shrimad Bhagavadgita*?

I have heard about a man who was a salesman of encyclopedias, a door-to-door salesman. He knocked at the door, a woman opened it and as he started his sales talk the woman said, "We already have a good encyclopedia; we don't need any. You can see: there in the corner on the table is the encyclopedia. So please forgive me, I am not interested."

The man said, "I can say definitely, that is not an encyclopedia; it is a *Bible*."

The woman said, "You seem to be a strange man—how can you say that so categorically?"

He said, "Because so much dust has gathered on it, nobody opens it." Encyclopedias are opened, people look into them, but who looks into *Bibles*? And he said, "I am ready to bet."

The woman said, "No there is no question, it is a *Bible*; just forgive me for telling you a lie."

Just the layer of dust was so thick, it was enough proof that it was not an encyclopedia but something holy. People are hiding all kinds of ugly things in *Holy Bibles*, holy *Gitas*, holy *Korans*.

The need is to make society aware that any kind of repression is against nature, to create a climate where what is natural is accepted, not denied. On the one hand, you will deny what is natural; then from some other door, your natural instinct will demand its satisfaction. That becomes a perverted need. In a very strange way, your so-called saints and your pornographers are in a conspiracy; they are both partners in the same business.

The saints go on telling people to repress sex, to be celibate. And these repressed people are hungry—you know if you have ever fasted, then the whole day you are thinking only about food and nothing else. You never think about food—every day you eat whatever you feel like eating and whatever your need is. You don't think about it, you don't dream about it, you don't need some pornography, some delicious dishes to look at. But I know people who have been on a fast...then their whole thinking becomes concentrated on food. They dream about delicious food; if you take them out in the market, they only see food stores, restaurants, hotels. They don't see anything else; nothing else is attractive.

It has been found in psychological experiments that if a man is kept for three weeks on a fast, he loses interest in seeing a pornographic picture. He would rather see a picture of a beautiful dish. It is not strange that people call women "beautiful dishes." It is humiliating, ugly, but somehow sex is also a hunger, as any other hunger is.

The problem becomes complex because people need pornography—if you provide pornography, you sell, you earn. If you don't provide it, the circulation of your newspaper or your magazine drops. You are in a very difficult dilemma: either you lose business or you have to do something which is absolutely ugly.

Unless the whole situation changes, unless the whole news media becomes aware of the fact, of why people are interested in pornography.... They should start creating an atmosphere—with articles, with stories, with poetry, with films, with television, with radio—that repression is anti-life. The day there is no repression in the world, there will be no need of pornography. The day there is no repression in the world, there will be no perversion, there will be no homosexuality, there will be no lesbianism.

And journalism has to become aware of the complexity of the situation. For example, now there is a great disease spreading all over the world—AIDS. It has come out of homosexuality. And the Catholic pope and other heads of religions are condemning homosexuality, but homosexuality is only a symptom. The real disease is the teaching of celibacy—because homosexuality was born in the monasteries, in soldier's camps, in boy scouts living together, in the hostels of boys and girls, which we have separated. Wherever we have separated man and woman, some kind of perversion arises.

In Texas, the government passed a law that homosexuality will now be a crime, punishable by five years in jail. And one million homosexuals—one would have never thought that Texas has so many homosexuals—one million homosexuals protested before the assembly hall. And these are not all the homosexuals of Texas, certainly—not everybody has joined in the protest. And they declared that "If you don't withdraw this law, we will go underground. There are gay restaurants, gay clubs, and all kinds of homosexual groups, openly—if you make it a crime we will go underground." And once homosexuality goes underground, then it will become more difficult to fight the disease that is being created by it.

The disease is spreading like wildfire, and every government of the world is trying to hide the fact of how many homosexuals there are in their countries, and how many homosexuals have tested positive for the AIDS virus. Because AIDS has no cure; the person is absolutely certain to die.

And scientists have shown with absolute certainty that we will not be able to find a cure. The disease is such that it is almost a slow death. It is not an ordinary disease; it has come out of behaving against nature, and nature is taking its revenge.

Just the other day, I was informed about South Africa: in one hospital they did a survey, just one month before—in the whole city, seventy percent of the prostitutes had AIDS. And after one month, when they did the survey the next time, a hundred percent of the prostitutes had AIDS. But this is not something to be surprised about; the more surprising fact which came to light was that out of all the mothers who came to give birth in the hospitals, seventy percent also had AIDS—the same percentage as the prostitutes. And these were not prostitutes, these were housewives... and their children will be born with AIDS. But the whole world is silent.

This is more dangerous than nuclear weapons, because nuclear weapons at least are something that can be controlled, something within our hands. But AIDS seems to be out of our hands.

The responsibility of the journalist is to bring before the people authentic facts, to make them aware how to avoid perversions. Homosexuality is not a disease; it is just a symptom of a disease. The real disease is celibacy, which is being preached by all religions. Now it is a strange game. The same people who are the cause of creating AIDS are condemning homosexuals. And they are the real criminals—if anybody needs to be behind bars, it is all your saints and all your preachers and all your priests. But not the homosexuals, they are victims—victims of an absolutely wrong psychology being preached for centuries.

Don't fulfill sick needs. Expose the fact that those sick needs are arising from a certain source. And create a protest in the minds of people so that the sources can be stopped. You cannot fight with the sick needs if the sources are not dropped. On the one hand you go on supporting the sources, and on the other hand you want people to drop their sick needs, which is impossible.

The fire and brimstone fundamentalist was ranting and raving before his congregation. "Praise the Lord, I know there are those among you who have committed the unspeakable sin of he-ing and she-ing. Stand up and repent!" Three-quarters of the congregation stood up.

"And there are those among you," continued the preacher, "who have committed that double sin of sins, he-ing and he-ing. Stand up and repent!" The rest of the men stood up.

"And I know there are those among you who have committed the triple sin, she-ing and she-ing. Stand up and repent!" The remaining women all stood up. No one was left sitting except one little boy with a puzzled look on his face.

"Preacher," he cried, "I would like to know where you stand on me-ing and me-ing?"

But this is the situation your religions have created. There is a great need for all these bogus, unscientific, unpsychological doctrines to be exposed to the public, and the public should be made aware to live a natural and healthy life, accepting whatever the need of the body is as a natural gift. Then only is there a possibility that we will be able not to exploit people's sick needs... because there will be no sick needs at all.

Journalism should not be only a business; it should also be a great responsibility towards humanity. It is no ordinary business, it cannot look only for profits. You have many other businesses for profit—at least don't corrupt journalism for the sake of profit. Journalism should be ready to sacrifice its profits; only then can it avoid fulfilling people's sick needs, and expose their original and basic causes—which can be removed.

Journalism should be a revolution, not just a profession. A journalist is basically a rebellious person—who wants the world to be a little better, who is basically a fighter—and he has to fight for right causes. I never look at journalism as just another profession. For profit, you have so many professions available; at least something should be left uncorrupted by the profit motive. Only then is there a possibility that you can educate people: educate them for a rebellious attitude against all that is wrong, educate them against anything that causes perversions.

One thing more I would like to remind you of. Life is not just a bed of roses, there are thorns too. But there is no need to make too much fuss about thorns. By making too much fuss about thorns, you slowly start forgetting about roses.

Journalism and other news media are a new phenomenon in the world. There was nothing like that in the times of Gautam Buddha or Jesus. That is one of the reasons that people go on bragging that the days of old were very beautiful. Hindu chauvinists go on saying that in the times of Gautam Buddha, people had no need to lock their doors. Their argument is that there was no stealing—but that is sheer stupidity, because Gautam Buddha preached every day for forty-two years against stealing. Do you think he was mad? If there was no stealing, to whom was he preaching, "Don't steal, don't lie"? All the teachings of all the old saints are against lying, against stealing, against adultery. You will not find anything new in the world that was not there before— you just have to look into their preaching.

If there were no locks, it is not because there were no thieves; in fact, there were no locks! And there was nothing to be locked, people were so poor. The lock is a certain stage of technology that was not there...and you have to have something to lock. You don't even have food for two meals a day—what are you going to lock?

It happened in Bengal in this century: Mahatma Gandhi was going on his tour towards Noachali, and a woman came and touched his feet and said, "Just wait a minute. My husband wants to touch your feet." So Mahatma Gandhi said, "But why has he not come with you?"

She said, "Don't make us embarrassed. We have only one good set of clothes, so I have come; now I will go and give the clothes to him and he will come. He's standing naked in the house."

This is in the twentieth century! We don't know about things that were happening which were evil in those times because there was no news media. The existence of news media has brought a very new thing—because everything evil, everything bad, everything negative, whether true or untrue, is sensational; it sells. People are interested in rapes, in murders, in briberies, in all kinds of criminal acts, riots. And because people are asking for all this news, you go on collecting all the wrong that is happening in the world. The roses are completely forgotten; only thorns are remembered—and exaggerated. And if you cannot find, you invent, because your whole problem is how to sell.

The same or even worse was the situation in the past, but people never came to know about it. They always knew about what can be called the "good news" because scriptures were written not about thieves, not about murderers, but about saints and their statements. That was the only literature. Journalism has brought the possibility of making saints out of criminals.

There was one case in Sweden...a man murdered a stranger whom he had never met; he had no idea who he was. He had not even seen his face. The man was sitting on the beach, looking at the ocean, and this other man came from behind and shot him dead. And in the court, the man said, "I wanted my picture to be printed on the front pages of all the newspapers. My desire is fulfilled. Now I don't care; you can sentence me to death, that's perfectly okay. My only desire was to see my picture in the newspapers." Now, you are creating a strange kind of person by the attention that you are paying to wrongdoings.

Last year a California university did a survey: after each boxing match, after each football match, the crime rate suddenly goes fourteen percent higher, and it remains fourteen percent higher for seven to ten days—then slowly it tapers down. But the government is not interested in preventing a barbarous thing like boxing—which is absolutely inhuman, and definitely inhuman to those two persons who are fighting. It creates in the whole state of

California fourteen percent more crimes: more murders, more rapes. Strange...still boxing continues, football matches continue. And the news media goes on reporting all these things. If the news media is alert, it should stop all commentaries on football matches, boxing—let them happen, but don't make so much fuss about them that the whole country becomes involved. They will die out by themselves.

The news media has to learn to boycott a few things which are creative of crimes, of inhumanity to human beings. But rather than boycotting them, you are flourishing, profiting from them, making your sales bigger and bigger, your circulation more and more, without ever giving a single thought to what the ultimate consequence is.

The old economics had the idea that wherever there is a need, there will be a supply. But the latest research shows that wherever there is a supply, slowly slowly the need is also created. For example, nobody needed a car five hundred years ago, nobody needed airplanes, nobody needed the railway.

When for the first time a railway train started from the London station, all the priests and bishops and cardinals and the archbishop of England gathered great congregations and declared: "This railway train was not made by God. When God created the world, it is obvious he never made the railway train, so who is making this railway train? It must be the devil."

And the old railway train, its engine, looked like the devil! The train was just experimental, only going for ten miles. The train was offering a free journey—breakfast, lunch, every comfort and luxury—to whoever wanted to come. And the preachers in every church were preventing people. What they were saying was, "In the first place, God never created it; in the second place, why are they persuading people by giving free tickets, breakfast, lunch, and all the comforts?"

"We can tell you," the archbishop told the congregation, "that this train will start, but it will never stop. So if you want to go, you can go. But remember, you will repent."

Nobody was ready to go into the train. A crowd was waiting all around the railway station, all along the ten-mile path, but nobody was ready. Only a few daredevils, thinking..."Let us see what happens. If it does not stop, so what? If they go on giving lunch and breakfast, let it not stop! What is the harm?"

A few people...the train was meant to carry one hundred and twenty people, but only eight people managed enough courage to enter the train. But once the train was there, it became an absolute need—now you cannot think of a world where trains don't exist, or cars don't exist, or airplanes don't exist.

Journalism not only has to look to fulfill the needs of the people, it has to create healthy supplies—which will create needs in people. That old law of economics is out of date...and that is the whole secret of advertisement. Why do people advertise? Particularly in America—the product will come two years afterwards, and advertisement starts two years before. They are simply making people aware of something which is coming into the market. The supply is first, and the supply is creating the need; hence, great advertisements are needed.

You can create better needs, healthy needs. You are not compelled to fulfill the sick needs of people. Fulfilling their sick needs is really committing a great crime.

But I have been around the world, and I have been puzzled that the so-called news media, if it cannot find something negative, invents it. All kinds of lies are invented. It never talks about anything beautiful, anything great. It does not create the idea in people that we are progressing, that we are evolving, that a better humanity is ahead. It only gives the idea that the night is going to be darker and darker.

And looking at your newspapers, your radio broadcasts, your television, your film, it seems that there is no way of going in any other direction than towards hell. Just in California alone...school kids are taking drugs—six year olds, eight year olds. Those days when there were hippies are gone—hippies have disappeared. Hippies were at least adult: twenty-one years, twenty-two, up to thirty. They are gone, they are no more. Now it is small school kids. There have been cases of murder by thirteen and fourteen-year-old boys, and there have been cases of rape by fourteen, fifteen-year-old boys. How does all this get into their minds? They see the films, and particularly the films that are prohibited to them—that prohibition becomes an invitation. They see in the news every day what is happening in the world.

In America alone, surveys show that every person is watching television for an average of seven hours every day—just glued to the chair for seven hours. And what is he watching? Murder, rape, robbery...slowly, slowly it gets into his head. He starts thinking, "This is all that is happening in the world; I'm just a fool who still goes to the church!" He never sees anybody praying, he never sees anybody meditating; he only sees people who are raping, people who are murdering: "Something must be wrong with me, I'm something abnormal. Normal people are doing normal things; all that I am doing is just being glued to the chair and watching television. Something has to be done." And slowly, slowly his mind is conditioned by all the input of the news media.

A healthy news media is a great need. And if you feel that perhaps this is not the need of the people, then create the need; create a beautiful supply. I don't think that there are not people who are going to be interested in the good side of life.

Don't take the attitude of a pessimist. There are people who are interested in the good side, there are people who are interested in the roses, there are people who are interested in all that is great in man. Bring it out; make everybody feel that if he is not doing something good, he is sick, abnormal. Right now just the opposite is the case.

Beloved Osho,

In our journalism training course, the growth of being, the spiritual dimension, is totally ignored, while other psychosomatic subjects are all very much highlighted. Osho, could You please explain: Why is it significant to include the spiritual dimension in the teaching of journalism?

Nandita, this country has been under slavery for two thousand years. That has created a psychological slavery in people. Although politically we are free, psychologically we are still slaves. Journalism is a product of the West, and we are imitating whatever is being done there; it is not our creation. The West does not believe in any spirituality, and it is suffering great anguish and great anxiety because of it.

The suicide rate is four times more than it is in the East. And in the East, people commit suicide because of hunger, starvation; you have to be compassionate towards them. In the West people commit suicide because they have everything, and they feel life is meaningless. They have all the money, they have all that money can purchase...but there are a few things which money cannot purchase. They cannot purchase silence, they cannot purchase joy, they cannot purchase love, they cannot purchase meditation....

In the life of Mahavira, there is a beautiful story. One great king of Mahavira's time, Prasenjita, had everything that was possible in those days. But one day he came across a Jaina monk who said to him, "You may be a great emperor, but do you know the blissfulness and the ecstasy of meditation?" And for the first time, Prasenjita was very shocked—he used to brag, thinking that he had everything. For the first time somebody had pointed out that he didn't have everything. He asked the monk, "From where can I get meditation?" He thought perhaps that too could be purchased. "I am ready to pay any price."

The monk said, "For that you will have to go to my master, who is living just outside the capital. You have to go to Mahavira."

Prasenjita went to Mahavira, and asked him the same question: "I have come here to purchase meditation, whatever the price. You don't be worried about the price—I am ready to pay right now—but I want meditation."

Mahavira looked at him, and said, "You certainly want meditation, but I don't want to sell it—at any price. But I know a very poor man in your own capital, my disciple. Perhaps he may be ready to sell it." Just a joke...so he gave him the name of the poor man, and he said, "Perhaps he may be in need of money, and he may sell his meditation."

And Prasenjita went in his golden chariot to the quarters of the poorest people, and they could not believe it—a great crowd gathered, and they found the poor man. Prasenjita asked, "Whatever the price, it will be given to you right now; I am carrying enough money in the chariot. But give me your meditation."

The man said, "My master must have been joking. It is not something that you can purchase. Although I am poor.... But it is not possible to sell meditation, you have to evolve into it."

In the West, four times as many people are committing suicide—and these people are not poor people, these people are from the highest class, super-rich. What is the problem, what is missing? And those who are not committing suicide are feeling at a loss. They have reached the highest rung of the ladder, and now...nowhere to go, and inside there is simply darkness and death.

Journalism is coming from the West. You are still copying something that has not grown within your culture, within your atmosphere; which is not part of this earth, it is not a flower here. So you are carrying a plastic flower; it has no roots.

In the West, the news media is not interested in spiritualism because in the West, nobody is interested in spiritualism. That has been their choice for centuries, and they are suffering because of it—badly suffering. So many people are in psychoanalysis, so many people are inside psychiatric hospitals, so many people are going insane, committing suicide, murdering, doing things just because they find life so meaningless, so useless.

One of the very famous novels of Dostoevsky, *The Brothers Karamazov*, has a statement by one of the brothers: If I meet God, I want to return my ticket. I don't want to be in the world; it is simply useless, there is no meaning.

You are asking me: "In our journalism training course, the growth of being, the spiritual dimension, is totally ignored." It is because you are not growing a journalism that belongs to this earth, that has the fragrance of this earth. You are simply imitating.

And you are doing a tremendous harm to this society, because here spiritualism is the most fundamental thing. But the same is happening in your educational systems. In your universities, in your colleges, in your schools, everywhere there is a mental slavery to the West. Whatever is happening in the West, you have to imitate it; it has become your unconscious habit. Journalism has to learn its own way, has to evolve its own individuality, just as education has to evolve its own individuality.

Nandita, you are asking if it is significant, and why it is significant to include the spiritual dimension in the teaching of journalism.

Spiritualism is the very meaning of life.

Without a spirit, a man is only a corpse. And without spiritualism, anything—education, journalism...they are only corpses, they stink.

Your politics is an imitation from the West. That's why even after forty years of freedom, nothing seems to have changed. The same bureaucracy...it has even got worse, because imitators cannot be better than the originals.

Your education is just an imitation. I have been a teacher in the university, and I had to fight with the university continuously. They were not ready to include yoga or meditation in the university courses, but they go on bragging that this is the land of Gautam Buddha and Mahavira and Bodhidharma and Patanjali and Kabir and Nanak—they go on bragging, but they don't see what they are doing. Their journalism, their education, their politics, has no trace of Kabir, or Nanak, or Patanjali, or Buddha.

They are under the impact of Western masters. Although politically you are free, psychologically you are not free.

Journalism has to attain freedom from the West and it has to give an authentic, original shape to itself. And you will be surprised that if you can manage to introduce a spiritual dimension to journalism, the West is going to imitate you sooner or later—because there is a great hunger, a great thirst. Rather than being imitators, why can you not be the originals, and let others be the imitators? That will be for the first time that something out of freedom happens in this country.

And spiritualism does not mean any kind of fanaticism. Spiritualism does not mean that you have to preach Hinduism, that you have to preach Jainism, or you have to preach Mohammedanism. Spiritualism simply means you have to spread the basic fundamentals of all religions, which are the same.

Can love be Hindu or Mohammedan? Can a peaceful mind be Hindu or Buddhist? Does a man of compassion have to be a Christian or a Jew?

An authentic spirituality will be without any adjective. It will teach only the essentials of all religions. And journalism should give it the first preference: on your laundry list, it should be your first item and politics should be the last. Unfortunately, politics is the first and spiritualism is not even the last.

I cannot understand how you can go on and on being slaves. Is not the time ripe that we should be spiritually free from the West? That we should have our own education, that we should have our own journalism? That we should have our own fragrance, and our own nuance?

The time is ripe, and journalism can become the beginning of a new era. Push politics as far back as possible, to the last pages of your newspapers. Politics is not our soul, it is the dirtiest game that you are propagating in people's minds. It is absolutely necessary that the politician be made clearly aware that he is not the man of wisdom, that he is not to guide the destiny of the nation; that he is only the servant of the people, his role is that of a functionary.

You don't make much fuss about who is the postmaster general; his role is that of a functionary. You don't make much fuss about who is the head of all the railways; what is the need? He is doing his work, he is getting his salary, that's enough. Why do you go on bothering about politicians? More than fifty percent of your energy is wasted on those whose life span is only four years. Tomorrow they will be forgotten.

They are exactly like your newspapers. Yesterday's newspaper is just as useless as your politician of yesterday.

But why give so much importance to momentary things? Spirituality means giving importance to something which is a permanent value, which gives life, light and guidance forever, which is *sanatan*, which is eternal. Eternal values constitute spirituality; momentary values constitute politics. Politics and religion are just polar opposites.

And politics is trying to make every effort to suppress religion in every part of the country. The only danger for politicians is from the religions, because only from the religions can people come out with more wisdom.

For example, I cannot see any problem so big that the country should remain struggling and not be able to solve it. Within ten years, every problem of this country can be solved. But the politicians don't want to solve the problems, they want to create them. In fact their very life depends on problems.

Adolf Hitler, in his autobiography, has a very significant statement: a politician, if he wants to be a great politician, a great leader of people, should never allow peace in his land. He should always create turmoil, keep people afraid, insecure, worried, concerned. He should keep people in such a situation that they need him. Always create enemies in the neighbors—real or phony, but always keep enemies on the side—and the moment you feel that your leadership is going, create a war, because only in war are great leaders born. And he is right. But what is the conclusion from it?

The conclusion is that the politician is not interested in solving problems, he is interested in making them as complex as possible. So he becomes absolutely essential; you need him always. He wants to keep you always afraid of the enemies—from China, from Pakistan—they are gathering atomic weapons, nuclear weapons, so you need your leaders, whether they are of any worth or not. In times of war, whoever is in power should be given total support, because it is a question of crisis. The cunning politician keeps every country always in crisis.

There is a saying that the first statement which can be called political was asserted by Adam to Eve. When they were driven out by God from the Garden of Eden, passing through the gate, Adam said to Eve, "We are passing through a great crisis." Since then, every politician has been saying the same thing: "We are passing through a great crisis." And the crisis is so great that only he can tackle it, you cannot manage it.

One of the greatest revolutions in journalism will be, Nandita, if we can create in this country a different kind of journalism—which is not dominated by politicians, but is inspired by its wise people. And you can remain absolutely certain that the wise people of any country are not going to fight in the elections; they are not going to beg for votes from the masses. So the wise people by their very nature remain out of power. It should be one of the basic functions of journalism to bring the wise people and their wisdom before the masses, into the light.

Politicians should not be paid too much attention; it is dangerous. They should be ignored as much as possible. They should be paid attention only when they do something which is authentically good.

Beloved Osho,

What is healthy journalism? Can journalism survive on positive news? Please explain Your vision on the responsibility of the media.

Nandita, by healthy journalism, I mean journalism which nourishes the whole personality of man—his body, his mind, his soul—journalism whose whole concern is to create a better humanity, not just to report what is happening. Journalism should not be just a news medium, it should also be great literature—then it is healthy. Even yesterday's newspaper should remain of some worth, so that even today it can be read. It should not be so momentary. But if you are only a news medium then naturally, once the day has passed, the news is old. You should make something that never becomes old, and always remains new.

That's what great literature is. Dostoevsky's novels, or those of Leo Tolstoy, Anton Chekhov, or Turgenev, Rabindranath Tagore...they will remain significant as long as humanity remains, and as fresh as ever.

Something in your journalism should have that quality, and that quality can be introduced. You can have space for news, but that should be secondary. Because what are those news reports? What are they going to do? Somebody steals—what is the point of reporting it? And somebody commits suicide—what is the point of reporting it? Why make it news unnecessarily? You are filling your space with absolutely nonessential things.

Bring the essential in. You have poets, you have painters, you have writers, you have spiritual giants—you can introduce all of them. They should be your major part, and politics should be just your third page, or fourth page—or maybe no page! You have made these politicians so huge, so exaggerated, and then the whole country suffers. The whole world is suffering because of these people, and you will have to take responsibility for it. These people should be cut down to size and put in their place. Somebody may be the president of the country; that doesn't mean much. The question is whether he is a great president; the quality is the question.

It happened when Abraham Lincoln became the president: The first day in the Senate, the aristocrats were very much arrogant and angry because he was not an aristocrat; he was the son of a shoemaker. And one aristocrat could not resist his temptation, and stood up. He said, "Mr. Lincoln, before you start your speech"—that was the inaugural speech—"I want you to remember that you are the son of a shoemaker."

The whole Senate clapped and laughed; they wanted to humiliate Abraham Lincoln. But you cannot humiliate a man like him. He stood silently and as the clamor died, he said, "I am very grateful to you, that you reminded me of my great father. I know my frailties, my weaknesses; I can never be as great a president as he was a great shoemaker. I stand as no comparison. My father was a great artist. I will try my best, but I know I cannot surpass him."

The Senate was shocked, but they recognized that this is not the kind of man whom you can humiliate. And he said to the man who had raised the question, "How have you remembered him? Because I remember perfectly well: my father used to go to your house also. Are you wearing the shoes made by my father? Are they pinching? Because I know something, I can mend them. I am not a great artist, but just by working with my father I have learned a little bit. So if any of you have any trouble with your shoes, you can always depend on me."

A president, just by being a president, is not much, but his quality... Talk of the qualities, don't talk of personalities. A prime minister, just by being the prime minister, does not mean anything. Talk about the qualities—what has he done to the country, what is he capable of doing? Provoke him to do it.

Days go on passing...I have seen these forty years passing. My whole family was involved in the freedom struggle, all of them had been in jails; we suffered as children. In my childhood I used to ask my father, "Are you certain that the freedom you are fighting for will ever come? It is possible that the British may go, but are you certain that the people who replace them will be better? I can understand that you are fighting against slavery, but I don't think you have any idea that you are fighting for freedom; you don't have any positive program."

The whole liberation movement in India was running without any positive program. And the result is that forty years have passed, and the country has been falling down and down. When I started speaking thirty years ago, the population of the country was four hundred million. I spoke in favor of birth control methods, and I was stoned, my meeting was disturbed. And next time when I reached that city, I was not allowed to get off the train. Two hundred Hindu chauvinists were standing on the platform; they would not let me get out.

And now the country's population has reached nine hundred million. By the end of this century it will pass one billion. For the first time in history, India will be ahead of China. Up to now, China was the most idiotic land; now India will be ahead of it. China has managed to cut its population, but your politicians don't have guts; they are afraid to tell the truth to people, because they have to get their votes.

Journalists should not be afraid of anybody; you are not dependent on anybody's votes. You should bring truth to the people: You are creating children—but in fact you are creating death. By the end of this century, half of the country—that means five hundred million people—will be dying of starvation: one man out of two. You will be surrounded by corpses. What are your politicians doing about it? And if I speak for birth control methods, then shankaracharyas condemn me, then the politicians try to destroy my efforts, because it goes against the religious superstitions of the people.

No politician has even the courage to come and meet me. Indira asked...six times she had appointments to come to me, and just one day before, she would cancel. Finally, I sent my secretary to ask her, "What nonsense is this? If you want to come, you come; if you don't want to come, nobody is inviting you. You have been asking...." And then she told my secretary, "My colleagues prevent me. They say if I go there, it is dangerous for my political future." Because I don't have any votes! The shankaracharyas and the imams and the bishops will all withdraw their votes, if they see a politician coming to me.

And it is one of the wonders that none of them is able to argue. I have been challenging them, saying that I am ready for a public debate with anybody on any point, and those cowards...none of them comes.

The journalists should bring to the public news of the people who are fighting for unpopular causes, because the unpopular causes are the future of man. The popular causes are the past, rotten heritage. The politician cannot have that courage, but the journalist can have it, and should have. Nandita, I call that journalism healthy.

And you are asking, "Can journalism survive on positive news?" I am not saying that; I am saying don't try just to survive on negative news. Bring out the positive, in all its beauty, and put the negative in the background; it should not be the focus. I don't want you just to be positive, I want you to be realists.

The negative side is a part of life, yes; death is a part of life. But that does not mean that you have to make your funeral ground in the middle of the market. You make your funeral ground outside the city, where you go only once and you don't come back. Why don't you make it in the middle of the bazaar so that everybody can see, passing by every day, that people are being burned?

It is part of life, so once in a while you can talk about the funeral, but don't focus on it. Death is certain, but life is more important. Talk about life, make life a celebration. Don't make people too much afraid of death.

Don't create a phobia with the negative; that's what I am saying. I am not saying that the media can survive only on the positive news—that will be wrong, that will be half. The negative should be brought to light, but should not be emphasized. It should be criticized.

The positive should be supported, and the negative should be condemned. In that way you are not being simply positive, you are bringing both...but the negative side is ugly. You know that in life we go on putting the negative out of the way, and we go on putting the positive in front. The same should be the attitude of a healthy journalism: the positive should be the goal. The negative should be used as a stepping-stone to it, but never emphasized, because that creates in people's minds the idea that the negative is what life is all about. That is a very dangerous cancer of the soul.

Beloved Osho,

What is Your trade secret?
Please make Your trade secret an open secret.

Nandita, I don't have any secret—but if you want to call it an open secret, then it can be described simply: I have been bringing the truth as I see it, without any fear of any vested interest. Whatever the consequences for me were, I have always accepted those consequences as rewards. And I have no regrets about life; I have lived it according to myself. Even if the whole world was against me I have never bothered to compromise.

You can call this my secret: I am a non-compromising man. Either I am true or I am wrong, and I fight for my truth, tooth and nail.

I have been around the world fighting for my truth, and it is hilarious to see that a single man can put the whole world against

him, and great nations like America and Germany and England
and Greece can freak out—and they don't have any answer.

I have been prohibited from entering twenty-one countries,
because they are afraid that if I enter their country for three weeks
I will destroy their morality, their religion, their tradition. I have
been asking, "If your religion, that you have been establishing for
two thousand years, is so poor that it can be destroyed in three
weeks' time, if your morality is so rotten that a single person on a
three-week tourist visa can demolish your morality, then it is
worth demolishing whether I come or not! You should do it
yourself."

And you will be surprised to know: countries like Germany
have even passed laws in their parliaments saying that I cannot
enter the country. I have never entered their country, and I have
never said that I wanted to enter their country. It is just from the
air, from nowhere. But the fear, the paranoia is spread all over the
world.

Other countries were doing the same—England did it,
America, then Germany. It was almost like wildfire, and they
forgot completely that at least you have to be intelligent in what
you are doing. Germany has passed a law that I cannot enter the
country, and not only that, my airplane cannot land at any airport
of Germany, for refueling or anything. They are afraid that
perhaps sitting in my airplane I can destroy and corrupt the people
of their land.

What a weak humanity we have.... Is this the country of great
intellectuals like Kant and Hegel and Feuerbach and Karl Marx?
Is this the country that has created really great thinkers...that is
afraid?

In Greece, I had a four-week tourist visa, and I had not gone
out of my house—I never go; whoever wants to come, comes. I
am just a well: if you are thirsty, you are welcome; if you are not
thirsty, the well is not going to run after you, because that would
be a very weird scene.

I had not gone out of the house. People were with me in the
house, twenty-five people, and those who wanted to come, were

coming to see me. The archbishop of the oldest church in the world, the Greek Orthodox Church, started a campaign against me. He said that if I were not thrown out from the country within twelve hours, the morality would be in danger, the religion would be in danger, the youth would be corrupted.

And these are the people who talk about peace, about love; they say "God is love," they talk about Jesus as "the prince of peace." The archbishop threatened the government, and he threatened me, that if within twelve hours I was not out of Greece, then he was going to dynamite my house with all the living people inside, and burn them all. Now, these are your religious leaders. The prime minister became afraid. The police came immediately...I was asleep, and my secretary stopped them and said, "Just wait, I will go in and wake him." But even the police were carrying dynamite, saying that "If you don't allow us, we will start dynamiting the whole place."

They threw my secretary, a young girl, from the first floor to the gravel on the ground, and dragged her into a jeep. I was asleep; I was awakened by the noise, because they started throwing stones and rocks against the beautiful palace that was my host's house. I could not understand what was happening, because I was sleeping on the second floor. And then one sannyasin came running, and he said, "The police seem to be absolutely mad! We were telling them that we were going to wake you up, but they have started throwing stones and breaking windows."

So I had to go down without even changing my clothes, and they said, "You cannot stay even for a single moment." No arrest warrant, no search warrant—and they forced me, at gun point. Forty loaded guns, against a man who has nothing in his hands, and who has not gone out of the house.

And I told the chief of the Greek police—because he was amongst the forty—"Now I can understand what kind of people poisoned Socrates. You must have been one of those people, born again."

I said, "Is there any reason for this? I have not done any crime, I have not done anything wrong against your society, I have not gone out of the house. And your morality is disturbed, your religion is disturbed." I have been around the world and I have seen the ugly faces...and the dead humanity.

I have enjoyed it immensely, hilariously, seeing that one man can put the whole world on fire—without having any dynamite in his hand, just with his words.

I don't have any secret—simply that I have been saying whatsoever I have felt as truth from the depths of my being. And I have been ready to fight for it in every possible way. If you think of that as a secret, Nandita, you can call it a secret; otherwise I am just a lover of stories, a storyteller. And through stories I have been demolishing people's superstitions as politely as possible.

Just the last thing....

A little girl was complaining to her mother about the long prayers she had to recite before going to bed at night.

"Why can't I say the short prayers that you and daddy use?" she asked.

"What prayers do you mean, sweetheart?" replied her mother.

"Well," said the little girl, "last night I heard Daddy say, 'Oh, dear God, I am coming!' and then you said, 'Lord, Jesus Christ, wait for me!'"

Okay, Maneesha?

Yes, Osho.

9

FRIENDLINESS IS ENOUGH

You have to live moment to moment, you have to live each moment as if it is the last moment. So don't waste it in quarreling, in nagging or in fighting. Perhaps you will not find the next moment even for an apology.

Beloved Osho,

Is the concept of soulmates more useful than marriage?

Prem Pragyan, one of the most significant things in man's life has been the love affair. Birth is not in your hands, death is not in your hands; and these are the only three great things in life: birth, love, and death. Only love is in your hands, only love gives you the freedom and dignity of being a human being; otherwise, birth and death happen just like any other animal, or any tree. Love should be kept as pure and unpolluted as possible.

You are asking, "Is the concept of soulmates more useful than marriage?" Concepts don't matter. What matters is your understanding. You can change the word 'marriage' to the word 'soulmates', but you are the same. You will make the same hell out of soulmates as you have been making out of marriage— nothing has changed, only the word, the label. Don't believe in labels too much.

Why has marriage failed? In the first place, we raised it to unnatural standards. We tried to make it something permanent, something sacred, without knowing even the ABC of sacredness, without knowing anything about the eternal. Our intentions were good but our understanding was very small, almost negligible. So instead of marriage becoming something of a heaven, it has become a hell. Instead of becoming sacred, it has fallen even below profanity.

And this has been man's stupidity—a very ancient one: whenever he gets into difficulty, he changes the word. Change the word 'marriage' into 'soulmates', but don't change yourself. And you are the problem, not the word; any word will do. A rose is a rose is a rose...you can call it by any name. You are asking to change the concept, you are not asking to change yourself.

Marriage has failed because you could not rise to the standard that you were expecting of marriage, of the concept of marriage. You were brutal, you were barbarous, you were full of jealousies, you were full of lust; you had never known really what love is. In the name of love, you tried everything which is just the opposite of love: possessiveness, domination, power.

Marriage has become a battlefield where two persons are fighting for supremacy. Of course, the man has his own way: rough and more primitive. The woman has her own way: feminine, softer, a little more civilized, more subdued. But the situation is the same. Now psychologists are talking about marriage as an intimate enmity. And that's what it has proved to be. Two enemies are living together pretending to be in love, expecting the other to give love; and the same is being expected by the other. Nobody is ready to give—nobody has it. How can you give love if you don't have it?

And when you feel that love is not coming towards you...and both feel the same: a great frustration and an idea, a suspicion that perhaps the other has deceived you. Before the marriage both were using beautiful words, sweet nothings; both were bringing their best to attract the other, to catch hold of the other. And once they are married, and the law has entered in, and society has granted you freedom to live together, soon the honeymoon is over. Even before coming back from the honeymoon it is over...all is finished because you have come to know the other in their total wholeness, which is ugly.

The facade, the mask that they were wearing before the marriage has slipped. You cannot hold it for twenty-four hours. When you live with someone, you have to come down from your hypocrisies and be whatever you are—and you know that you are not the person you pretend to be. The same is true about the other. And then it becomes a struggle to possess the woman, to possess the man.

The only significant symptom of love is, it never possesses; on the contrary, it gives freedom. It is happy in the happiness of the other. It does not beg; it is not a beggar. It is an emperor. It gives, and it gives unconditionally.

But in actual life, what we have been doing for centuries is asking the other to give; and the other is also asking you to give. And both are beggars, their bowls are empty; they don't have anything to give. It becomes a struggle, a warfare.

You can change the concept from marriage to soulmates, but what about you? What about the people who will become soulmates? If they are the same people who were becoming a couple in a marriage, nothing will change.

My suggestion is, neither marriage is needed nor soulmates are needed—just friendliness is enough. You don't know anything about soul, how can you become a soulmate?

If you can become just friendly with each other, that is more than can be expected from the present man. If you can be understanding of each other's frailties, weaknesses, that is more than can be expected.

If you can drop the old superstitions, that once a woman or a man loves you, they have to love you forever... Love is very fragile. It is just like a flower: beautiful, but very delicate. In the morning it blossoms; by the evening it is gone, its petals are scattered. That was a beauty in the morning; by the evening it has become a grave. Life is a changing, continuously changing phenomenon.

When I say a great understanding is needed, the old idea of permanent relationship under any concept has to be dropped. You have to live moment to moment, you have to live each moment as if it is the last moment. So don't waste it in quarreling, in nagging or in fighting. Perhaps you will not find the next moment even for an apology.

One of the mystics, Sarmad, used to tell his disciples every night, "We are going to sleep for the last time. Please forgive me. As a master I may have been hard to you. I had to be because I loved you and I wanted a transformation to happen. And I don't know whether in the morning I will wake up again, so I'm asking for your forgiveness." Each night he would go to bed as if it was the last night—and one day it is going to be true, one night will be the last night and you will never wake up again.

And each morning he would wake up as if it was a new beginning; he had accepted death in the night before, now this was a rebirth. He looks tremendously grateful towards existence: one day more to live, one day more the sun, the wind, the trees, the birds, one day more of friends, one day more of love. But not more than that.

The very idea of having a permanent, lifelong relationship helps you to postpone that which is essential and go on doing things which are absolutely nonessential; not only nonessential but idiotic.

People are fighting about such small things that they themselves, in their saner moments, laugh about it. I have heard about a couple who were getting married in the government registrar's office. The man signed—the woman had signed before him. As she saw the man's signature, she immediately told the registrar, "I want a divorce." The registrar said, "What has happened? You are getting married, you have just signed the marriage papers."

She said, "Yes, I have signed but things have gone sour already. Just look at the paper. I have signed in small letters and he has signed in such big letters, to show me who he is. This is the beginning of trouble—I don't want to get into it." The bigger letters already declare the supremacy, superiority of the man.

You can change words—I would like to change your consciousness.

The idea of permanent relationship was wrong, but it has been imposed on you by poets, by priests, by everybody. And I am not saying that two persons cannot live in deep friendship for their whole life. They can, but it should not be a conditioning, but just a flowering of friendship, open. Any day one partner can say, "I am grateful for all the beautiful moments you have given to me, but now our paths separate. In sadness...but I will remember you always. I don't want life with you to create a hell. Then all that was beautiful will be destroyed, even the memory of it will be destroyed. Just a friendliness is enough."

My vision of a new society is that of small communes, not of big cities. A commune consisting of not more than five thousand people, so that people can know each other very easily. And the commune should take the whole responsibility for the children, and nobody should be allowed to have children unless the commune needs them. That decision will be of the commune. And now all scientific techniques are available. The society can decide what it needs—engineers, doctors, scientists, poets, mystics. Now it is scientifically possible to choose what kind of a child you are going to give birth to, you just have to drop your old superstition that the child has to be yours.

Just as you have blood banks, you should have sperm banks in every hospital. And scientists are able now to figure out about every living sperm; they can read it, what it is going to be. Up to now we have lived a very accidental life, and perhaps the world is so full of stupid and retarded people because of that.

When two persons make love, the man releases in one lovemaking almost a million living sperm, and a great politics starts because they all run fast to reach the mother's egg. Only one will be able to enter. The mother's egg is made in such a way that it remains open until a living male sperm has entered it. The moment the sperm enters, it closes. It rarely happens that two cells reach simultaneously—that's why twins are born—or sometimes three, or sometimes four; but these are exceptions.

That small passage is a long journey for the small sperm. According to its size it is almost two miles long, and a great struggle...a million people trying to reach to become the president! My understanding is that the wiser ones will stand to the side and let the idiots go ahead.

Rabindranath was the thirteenth child of his parents. If there had been birth control, Rabindranath would not have ever been born. And even without birth control there are very few people who produce thirteen children. If the parents had stopped at one dozen, which would have been more logical and a more rounded figure, Rabindranath would have been out of the game, you would never have heard of that man and his greatness.

But science has become able, within these last ten years, to read the whole future of a single sperm: whether it is going to become a scientist, whether it is going to become a poet or a doctor or a philosopher or a mystic or a dancer or a musician. Its potential can be read. Its life pattern, in minute detail, can be read: whether it will be a healthy child or a sick child, whether it will die after six months or after a hundred years. To go on doing the old accidental thing and producing children, not knowing whom you are bringing into the world—whether you are giving birth to an Adolf Hitler or a Benito Mussolini or a Joseph Stalin or a Ronald Reagan...you don't have any idea. It is a very blind game.

Love should be only of friendship. And if society has a need and the medical profession proves your wife to be the right vehicle for bringing a child into the world, then from their sperm bank they can find the right sperm and inject it. You can go on making love; that is a separate affair.

There has been the pill, but it was not a hundred percent foolproof. Sometimes you are not thinking that you are going to make love and you don't take the pill, and suddenly your lover turns up and you take the risk. They chance it—it is not always that one becomes pregnant. Now they have come up with two other pills. One is to be taken after you have made love—that is a hundred percent effective—and for the second one the woman is not needed, just the man can take a pill. They have come up with a pill for men, too. Then the woman need not take any pill. Your love becomes pure fun, pure joy, without any responsibility and burden.

And the woman should be educated, should be given all the opportunities to become an independent individual, financially and in every other respect, so that she is no longer dependent on you. An independent woman and an independent man, just out of friendship feel good to be with each other. As long as they feel good they remain together. The moment they feel things are going wrong, there is no need to prolong the affair. They can say good bye with gratitude towards each other. No law is needed, no government permission, no social sanction is needed—because who are these people to interfere in your life?

Yes, society can only have a concern about the children because that is going to be the future society. Society cannot allow you to produce Adolf Hitlers. But society has not done anything to prevent it. And this can be prevented.

There is no need of calling it marriage or soulmates or any great words...just hot air! Use simple words. You feel friendly towards someone and you feel joyous to be with the person. As long as you feel joyous it is valid. The moment trouble arises, you can separate. Marriage has created so much ugliness in the world, that you cannot conceive.

First, it has given accidental generations which are not produced out of understanding, out of a scientific approach, but just like animals, under the force, the blind force of biology; otherwise we can have so many beautiful people around. And the world does not consist only of a beautiful moon and beautiful stars, its greatest beauty is a beautiful person: physically, mentally, spiritually.

The by-products of marriage have been very strange. All religions are against prostitutes, but they are a by-product of marriage. In fact, prostitutes are a safety measure for marriage to remain, because by nature neither man is monogamous nor woman is monogamous. Monogamy is a kind of bondage, imprisonment. Why should you be so one-dimensional when life has given you all the opportunities of multidimensionality? No one can say whether tomorrow you may come across a woman and you may fall in love.

The society in a subtle way approves of prostitutes. It is an arrangement for men, when they get bored with their wives. And wives also have been accepting, down the ages, the existence of the prostitute because they know the prostitute is only a commodity, she is not a competitor. The husband may go there for one day, that's all. She becomes more worried when the husband falls in love with some woman; then there is competition. With the prostitute there is no competition.

Prostitutes used to come to rich houses to dance and to give pleasure to the rich people, and it was accepted. The wife was not at all disturbed by it—because she is only a purchased woman, she will be gone tomorrow. It is not going to be a constant problem for her. But the woman was completely confined in monogamy. It is only just now, because of the women's liberation movement in Europe and in America, that male prostitutes have become available. Now woman can also have the same opportunity that man has enjoyed for thousands of years. It is strange and ugly, but because we are going against nature we have to find some way to satisfy nature.

Polygamy is the nature of man and woman both, because polygamy is multidimensional, it is a freedom. If today I love someone and tomorrow I find someone who suits me more, then why should I be prevented? If tomorrow I find someone who is more harmonious with me, then why should I be prevented and kept in bondage? And of course, in this bondage I will be suffering and it will be a torture, and I will take revenge on the poor woman who has done nothing to me.

So one thing: the old superstition that love is monogamous has to be dropped—it is not. There is every evidence against it.

Secondly, the old superstition that love has to be permanent, only then is it true, is absolutely wrong. If a roseflower is not permanent, do you think it is not real? And if you are so much interested in permanency, then you can have only plastic flowers, not real roses. Those plastic flowers don't die because they don't have any life, they are already dead. Love is a very living phenomenon. In fact, life comes to its highest peak in love.

Hence, there is every possibility that what has been today a great blessing, tomorrow may not be there. It is a breeze that comes and goes. We have to accept nature as it is. To create something unnatural is going to create perversions.

"I locked my husband out of the house last week for playing around with other women," confessed the attractive young housewife. "And now he wants me to take him back. What should I do, Father?"

"You must take him back, it is your Christian duty," replied the priest, patting her hand. "But," he added as his grip tightened, "how would you like to get even with the bastard?"

After all, your priest is also a human being. You have forced him into celibacy, so he has to find ways... Fifty percent of the monks in a Christian monastery in Ethos have declared that they are homosexuals and they are going to remain homosexuals. You will be surprised to know that the archbishop of England has been considering a petition from many cardinals that homosexuality should be allowed, it is not against celibacy. A great idea!

The idea is that celibacy is only against heterosexual relationships. Homosexual relationship is not the question; it does not break the vow of celibacy. These poor priests, they are hung up in an unnatural situation. Naturally, they have to find some way through the back door. And they are enforcing unnaturalness on other people.

I have heard about a party of very super-rich people...because the more rich you become, the more open you become with your perversions. You can afford it. The poor man will be condemned and crushed, will lose his job, but who can raise a finger against the super-rich? They have their private theaters in their own homes, where they can see blue movies. For them, special movies are created, absolutely ugly, of sex orgies.

There was a party of very super-rich people and they were playing a game, and the archbishop of the country was also invited. The game was so strange that the archbishop said, "I feel that I should retire. I cannot join in the game." He had come a little late so he had no idea that the game had already been going on.

The game was that the lights would be turned off and all the men would stand naked and the women would find out, by touching their genitals, who the person was. If they can guess the right name, then they have the right to have the night with the person.

The archbishop said, "This goes against my religious ideology and I cannot participate." But the people laughed. They said, "Don't be a hypocrite, the game has been going on and your name has been proposed three times. All the women seem to know you perfectly well, so don't feel shy."

All these uglinesses are by-products.

Two little old ladies were chatting over the back yard fence. The first one boasted, "I went out with old man Cane last night and I had to slap him twice."

"To stop him?" asked the friend.

"No," she giggled, "to start him up."

He must be too old, maybe falling asleep. She had to slap him so he came to his senses...what is he doing?

If you look at the back doors, it is a very hilarious situation. Marriage has proved ugly because it has perverted people into homosexuality, into sodomy, into all kinds of perversions, into pornography. It has given them the opportunity to make women slaves. Half of the population of the world has been deprived of all kinds of spiritual growth.

Women have asked again and again why there are not women as great as Gautam Buddha or Jesus or Zarathustra or Lao Tzu. Man has not allowed women even to be educated. He has not allowed women to have any financial independence. He has not allowed the woman free movement in society. At the most she can go to church. The only man available to her is the priest.

How can the woman become a Gautam Buddha? Gautam Buddhas don't grow on trees; neither they drop from the sky suddenly! They need roots in the earth and they need nourishment to grow. The woman, in the past particularly, has been continually kept pregnant. She has been used like a factory for reproduction. And it was a biological necessity, because out of ten children, nine were dying and only one was surviving. So if you needed a few children, the wife had to be continually pregnant. There was no time for her to be a Gautam Buddha. She was not even accepted as equal to man.

Marriage has created the family: the unit of the society, the unit of the nation. Unless the family disappears, nations cannot disappear. And without the disappearance of nations, wars will continue, man will continue to butcher man. To me, marriage is one of the things that needs to be immediately abolished. With marriage abolished, prostitution will disappear. And everybody is miserable—husbands are miserable, wives are miserable.

I have been staying with thousands of families—everybody is miserable. And because I have been loved by so many people, the husband could open his heart to me, the wife could open her heart to me. Both are beautiful people, but together they are continuously at war. Every house has become a battlefield. And children are growing in this poisonous atmosphere. They will learn the same techniques and strategies and they will repeat them.

That's how every generation goes on giving its diseases to the new generation. Generations change, diseases have become permanent. Now we have to drop the diseases, so that the future humanity can be free from all this ugliness.

Don't just give it a new name, change it from the very foundations.

Three young men arrived at the pearly gates together and St. Peter asked, "How did three healthy men like you die so soon?"

"Well," said the first, "it happened like this: I came home from work early one day and found my wife stark naked in bed, the bedcovers all a mess. I saw her glance at the open window, and so I looked out and saw a man running across the front yard. I raced into the kitchen, picked up the fridge, carried it back to the bedroom and hurled it out of the window at the running man. But unfortunately the effort was too much for me and I died."

"What about you?" St. Peter said to the second man.

"Well," he replied, "I don't know what the hell happened. I was late for an appointment so I ran out of my ground floor apartment and some idiot dropped a fridge on my head and I died."

"And what about you?" said St. Peter to the third man.

"Well, Pete," said the man shyly, "it all started when I was in the fridge."

This is going on.... It is a hilarious situation.

Before she left her friend's house one evening, aunt Emma was warned that a sex maniac was loose in the neighborhood. When she returned to her apartment, she cautiously looked under the bed, in her closet, and behind her curtains. Then Emma switched on the light.

"Well," she sighed, "he is not here, damn it!"

Beloved Osho,

What is sleep for You? Do You leave Your body while it is resting or does sleep help You to stay in Your body?

Prem Shunyo, asleep or awake, my consciousness is in the same state. To me, sleep is samadhi. That's how Patanjali explains samadhi: a sleep without dreams; a sleep which is not unconscious, which is not like a coma, but simply a light rest for the body. But deep inside, the inner being is fully alert...just like a candle burning all night in a dark room, where no wind comes in. It remains unwavering but goes on radiating light.

I don't feel any difference in my sleep or in my awakening. The same light and the same blissfulness and the same silence continues day in, day out. My sleep is not much of a sleep, just a thin layer of rest for the body. Inside I am all awake.

You are asking, "Do you leave your body while it is resting or does sleep help you to stay in your body?" I don't leave my body while I am asleep and neither does sleep help me to remain in the body. In fact sleep helps my body to continue functioning. My inner being, my subjectivity is awake all the time. I don't have any dreams because I don't have any repressions of anything. I am not an ascetic, I am against all repressions. I am the most natural man possible—almost wildly natural.

Sleep is also a beautiful experience of tremendous rest. You feel the aftereffects of rest in the morning, when you wake up. It is only inference for you that sleep must have refreshed you, must have taken away all tiredness, must have rejuvenated you; but these are your inferences. To me, these are my eyewitness experiences. While the body is resting, relaxing, regaining its strength, I am watching it. It is not in the morning that I find my body is relaxed, I find it relaxed simultaneously as it is resting. And there is no need to leave the body.

My work is of a totally different kind. I don't want to interfere in anybody's life; otherwise it has been done, it can be done: one can leave the body and while somebody else is asleep, can work upon the person. But it is an infringement of somebody's freedom, and I am absolutely against any infringement, even if it is for your good, because to me freedom is the ultimate value.

I respect you as you are, and because of my respect I go on telling you that much more is possible. But that does not mean that if you don't change, I will not respect you. That does not mean that if you change, I will respect you more. My respect will remain constant, whether you change or not, whether you are with me or against me. I respect your humanity and I respect your intelligence.

Rather than working in a way in which you will not be conscious, my work is absolutely to confront you consciously. And my experience is that this way is the best way and the right way. Coming from the back door in your sleep and changing things, in the first place is a criminal offense—although nobody can see the crime or catch the criminal, because it is absolutely invisible. You will never know, but the change that will happen to you will always remain something foreign, as if it has been imposed on you, and you will feel a certain tension.

I can make you more loving by coming to you in your sleep. And you will become more loving but your love will have a certain tension, it will not be relaxed, because you have not really changed; it has not come from your own understanding. It has to come consciously from your own understanding. So my work has a very different approach. I go on talking to you, making every effort that you listen and you understand, and if something comes out of that, it is your own. And what is your own is the only real treasure.

Hymie Goldberg was down on his luck, so he went to the local synagogue and approached the rabbi. "All I need is fifty dollars to get me out of debt," sobbed Hymie. "I keep praying to God but he does not answer my prayers."

"Don't lose faith," said the rabbi. "You must keep praying." After Hymie left, the rabbi began to feel sorry for him. "I don't make much money," he thought, "but that poor man needs help. Perhaps I will give him twenty-five dollars out of my own pocket."

The next day the rabbi went to Hymie's house and handed him an envelope with twenty-five dollars inside and said, "Here, Hymie, God has sent this for you."

After saying good bye to the rabbi, Hymie closed the door, looked inside the envelope and bowed his head. "But next time you send money," he said to God, "please send it directly to me. That bastard rabbi kept half of it!"

Things should be done directly, with your understanding; otherwise there is going to be a mess, a conflict. I can give you some change, but it will not have roots in you. So it will be something polished, just on the surface. Deep inside you will be still carrying your old garbage.

A drunk walked into an open elevator shaft and fell twenty-four stories straight down. Shakily he stood up, brushed himself off, carefully adjusted his hat and shouted, "Damn, I said 'Up!'"

In your unconsciousness, in your sleep, I don't want to disturb you. My approach is purely of individual respect and respect for your consciousness, and I have immense trust in my love and in my respect towards your consciousness, that it will change you. And that change will be authentic, total, irreversible.

Okay, Maneesha?

Yes, Osho.

10

GENETIC SCIENCE: FOR THOSE WHO LOVE CREATION

Go forwards and learn some lesson from the past so that, as scientific technology develops, simultaneously human consciousness should develop. And that will be the protection against technology being used as something harmful to mankind.

Beloved Osho,

I heard You speak of scientists choosing future people from their genetic analysis of sperms. I have no trust in scientists, or doctors or anybody whose knowledge extends no further than their head. I intuitively feel that genetics plays only a small role in determining what a person becomes. A gardener may well have become a musician; a soldier may have the potential to be a scientist. Surely what a man is, is no measure of what he might have been in different circumstances.

Beloved Master, who could have foreseen an Osho in the sperm and egg of Your father and mother? Please speak more on the underlying sanity behind Your suggestion—which I cannot see because of my fear of totalitarian regimes.

Devageet, I can understand your concern; it is my concern too. But there are many things to be understood. The first is, never act out of fear. If man had acted out of fear there would have been no progress possible.

For example, the people who invented bicycles...can you ever think of any danger? It is simply inconceivable that bicycles can be dangerous. But then the Wright brothers made the first flying machine out of the parts of bicycles. The whole world rejoiced— because nobody could have foreseen that airplanes would be used to destroy cities, millions of people, in the first world war.

But the same airplanes are carrying millions of people around the world. They have made the world small, they have made it possible to call the world just a global village. They have made bridges between peoples, they have brought together people of different races, religions, languages in such a way that no other invention has been able to do. So the first thing to remember is that acting out of fear is not the right way.

Act cautiously, with consciousness, remembering the possibilities and the dangers, and creating the atmosphere to prevent those dangers. Now, what can be more dangerous than nuclear weapons in the hands of the politicians? You have put the most dangerous thing into their hands.

Now, in fact there is no need to be afraid; even nuclear weapons can be used creatively. And I have a deep trust in life, that they will be used creatively. Life cannot allow itself to be destroyed so easily, it is going to give tremendous resistance. In that resistance is hidden the birth of a new man, of a new dawn, of a new order, of the whole of life and existence.

According to me, nuclear weapons have made a great war impossible. Gautam Buddha could not do it, Jesus Christ could not do it. All the saints of the world together have been talking about nonviolence, no war; they could not succeed. But nuclear weapons have done their job.

Seeing that the danger is so big, all the politicians are trembling deep down, that if a third world war begins the whole of life will be destroyed—and they will be included in it. They cannot save themselves. Nothing can be saved. This is a great chance for all those who love creation. This is the moment when we can turn the whole trend of science towards creativity.

Remember one thing: that science is neutral. It simply gives you power. Now, how to use it depends on you, depends on the whole of humanity and its intelligence. Science gives us more power to create a better life, to create more comfortable living, to create more healthy human beings—rather than preventing...just out of fear that some totalitarian power may misuse it.

Everything can be misused. And Devageet himself is a doctor; he himself belongs to the category of scientists. He should understand one thing, that everything that can harm can also be of tremendous benefit. Don't condemn anything, just raise the consciousness of human beings. Otherwise you are falling into the same fallacy into which Mahatma Gandhi has fallen.

Once you start acting out of fear, where are you going to stop? Mahatma Gandhi was using the same logic, and he stopped at the spinning wheel. That must have been invented at least twenty thousand years ago and he did not want to go beyond that. He wanted everything that has been invented after the spinning wheel to be destroyed. He was against railway trains, because in India railway trains have been used to make the whole country a slave.

These railway trains in India were not created for people's comfort and their service. They were created to move armies, so that within hours armies can move from one part of the country to another part. This is a vast country. There are places which, even by railway train, you can only reach in six days' time. It is almost a subcontinent; and to control this country they had to spread a big network of railway trains. Its basic purpose was the army and the army's movement.

But that cannot make us decide that railway trains should be destroyed. That would mean the movement of man is curtailed, he falls back into the Dark Ages. Mahatma Gandhi was not in favor even of innocent things like telegrams, telegraphs, the post office, because they were all used in India, in the beginning, to control the country. Slowly, slowly they were changed into public services. Every invention has been used first by the military, by the war-mongers, and finally they have come to be used by the people.

What is needed is not to go backwards; otherwise you will destroy the whole humanity. What is needed is to go forwards and learn some lesson from the past: so that, as scientific technology develops, simultaneously human consciousness should develop. And that will be the protection against technology being used as something harmful to mankind.

My basic disagreement with Mahatma Gandhi has been this: that he was dragging humanity backwards.

First, horses were used by the soldiers. Do you mean to say that horses should not be used any more? In fact, every vehicle has been used in the beginning in the service of death. Now there are all kinds of medicines; and allopathic medicines—which is the official science in the world as far as medicines are concerned— are mostly poisons. They are in the hands of the powerful.

Now there has been great concern that the Soviet Union is developing a certain ray called a death ray. It can be extracted from the sunrays; it does not reach us because there is a certain layer of ozone around the earth which prevents it from entering. Ozone turns the death rays back.

But we only became aware of it when our first rockets went to the moon. They made holes in the ozone layer and death rays entered. And immediately the cancer rate went so high that it was unbelievable—what has happened? And then it was found that there are some rays reaching the earth which have never been reaching before. The Soviet Union has been trying to generate those death rays rather than sending nuclear weapons and missiles and airplanes loaded with bombs without pilots, controlled just by remote control.

They are trying to find a far more refined way. Just sending rays...you cannot do anything against those rays, they are not even visible. And they will not destroy anything, houses will remain intact. They will simply destroy only living things—man, birds, animals, trees, anything that has any kind of life. The moment the death ray touches it, life disappears. It will create really a tremendous nightmare. Houses will be there, streets will be there, shops will be there, everything will be there, just life will not be there.

But even then I would not say, not to investigate death rays. As the Russians began to work on death rays, America immediately started to work on how to prevent them, how to detect them, how to turn them back, how to create anti-death rays. And there is a possibility... Perhaps in the future, even if man does not use these things, if the ozone layer starts breaking in different parts and death rays enter into the atmosphere, we will be able to create anti-death rays to turn them back. We may be able to create, closer to us, another ozone layer.

So one should not act out of fear; one should see the whole perspective. If there is fear, that means the fear comes not from the power generated by science, the fear comes from the unconscious man. In his hands everything becomes poisonous, dangerous.

Change the man, don't stop progressive science. For example, what I have told you was the latest findings of genetic scientists. Up to now we have lived accidentally, in the hands of blind biology. You don't know what kind of child you are going to give birth to—blind, retarded, crippled, ugly; and he will suffer his whole life. And in an unconscious way you are responsible, because you never bothered to figure out some way that only healthy children—not blind, not deaf, not dumb, not retarded, not insane—are born.

And particularly now, when children are born with AIDS, you have to take some steps to choose which children should be born and which children should not be born. The children born with AIDS are bringing death to themselves, to their family, to their friends. They will go to the schools, they will go to the colleges, and they will spread it. And finally they will get married, and they will produce children who will have AIDS.

Now, unless we listen to the genetic scientists, there is no way to prevent it. Devageet is perhaps not aware that genetic science is able to exactly figure out a few things: for example, whether the child born out of a certain combination of male and female energy is going to be healthy or not.

In Tibet, in the past they used a very strange method, very primitive; but you cannot be angry against them, they had to use it. It was a very barbarous method. Whenever a child was born, immediately it was dipped in ice-cold water seven times. Out of

ten children, nine children used to die—the ice cold water...
Immediately after the child is born, the first thing is to dip him into
ice-cold water. He will become blue by the seventh time; you are
just dipping a corpse.

But it was absolutely necessary, because Tibet is the highest
land in the world, at the top of Himalayas. Life is very hard, it
needs very strong people, and the cold is killing. Unless a child is
able to cope, it is better he dies. It was out of compassion, not out
of cruelty. It is better that he dies rather than suffer his whole life.
He will not be able to function, will not be able to work. And the
land needs people who can tolerate that much cold and still work,
produce. This was an ancient type of genetics. They were
choosing—although they had no idea how to do it. But somehow
they managed to choose the healthiest people.

Hence the outcome has been that Tibetans have lived the
longest, because all the people who would have died in the middle
somewhere have been finished on their first entry into the world.
They were returned unopened! And the people who remained
were really strong, really stubborn. They have lived a long life and
a very healthy life, because they eliminated all the weaklings from
the very beginning. And it was part of compassion. Why allow a
person to live who is going to suffer his whole life from all kinds
of diseases, sicknesses, weakness? He will not be able to enjoy life
at all.

Genetic scientists cannot say in detail that this man will
become a doctor, or an engineer, or a gardener, but they can say a
few things very definitively and a few things as possibilities.
About health they can say very definitively; what kind of diseases
the child will suffer from they can say very definitively. So
precautions can be taken, and the child can be saved from
suffering from those diseases. They can certainly and very
definitively say how long the child will live. Measures can be
taken to prolong his life.

On the side of possibilities, they can say that this child has a
possibility, a potential for being a musician. That does not mean
that he cannot become a doctor; that simply means that if the right

opportunities are given to him he will become a musician rather than becoming a doctor. And if he does not become a musician and becomes a doctor, he will never find fulfillment. His innermost being will remain missing something.

So if the genetic scientist can say that these are the possibilities, the society, the parents, the commune, can make certain opportunities available to the child. Right now, we don't know what his potential is. We have to decide; parents are in a dilemma where to send the child: to an engineering college, to a medical college, to a carpentry workshop, or to a car mechanic. Where to send him, and how to decide? Their decision comes out of financial considerations. That is the only way for them to decide—which way the child will be a success financially, comfortable, prestigious. That may not be the potential of the child, but parents have no idea.

The genetic scientists can simply give you the possibilities. They are not saying these are certainties, that whatever you do this child will become a musician. They are not saying that, because nature can be diverted by nurture. If you stop all possibilities for him to become a musician and you force him to become a doctor, he will become a doctor; but he will be a doctor his whole life unwillingly, without any joy.

Nurture is important, but if we know exactly what the possibilities are, we can help the child through the right kind of nurture. Then nature and nurture can function harmoniously together and create a better human being, more contented with himself, more joyous, and creating a more beautiful world around him.

Only on one point are you right: genetics is capable of giving the potential about everything except enlightenment, because enlightenment is not part of a biological program. It is something beyond biology.

Hence, in genetic science there is no way to say that this person is going to become enlightened. At the most they can say this person will have a leaning more towards spirituality, mysticism, more towards the unknown; but if these leanings are known, we can provide the nurture for him. And the world will have more enlightened people than has ever been possible before.

The fear that Devageet feels is that if genetics falls into the hands of totalitarian governments, they will start choosing children who will be obedient to the status quo, who will not be revolutionaries, who will never become rebellious, who will be always ready to become slaves without any resistance.

That fear is there, but that fear can be avoided. Why give the power to totalitarian governments? I am giving you a whole program for society.

My first idea is, nations should disappear. There should be a world government which is only functional. And there is no problem of its being afraid about revolution because it will be a servant of the people. And the functionaries of the world government will be only a Rotary Club. They will go on changing each year. Nobody will be in power for more than one year, no one will be allowed to be in power in the government again.

Only one time, for one year—what can he do? And his power is not totalitarian. The people who have chosen him have the right to recall him at any moment. Just fifty-one percent of the voters who have chosen him give a signature to the government that they want him to be recalled—he is going against the interest of the people—and the person loses all his power. His power is not given to him for five years without any restraint. Anyway he is going to be out of power at the end of the year, and he will never see power again, so he will make the most of it, to do something that will make him be remembered. And if he tries to do any harm, we have the possibility of recalling him. Just fifty-one percent of the voters are needed to sign a petition and the person can be out.

My plan is complete for the whole society; it is not fragmentary. Big cities, by and by, should disappear; small communes should take their place. Families should disappear, so there is no loyalty towards a family, no loyalty towards a nation. Children are brought up by the commune, not by the parents. And it is to be decided by the commune how many children are needed, because as people's lives become longer we will need less and less children. If the old people are going to stay longer, then for new guests we don't have any room.

In the past it was possible—go on producing children, as many as you can. A woman was almost always pregnant, until the day she became unable to be pregnant. She went on producing like a factory—because people's life span was very small.

The findings are that five thousand years ago, nobody lived more than forty years. Not a single skeleton has been found, of this age, in the whole world, which has been proved to be more than forty years old. When a man died, he was not more than forty years old—and this may be the highest age limit, not the average. When people were dying at thirty-five years or forty years of age, naturally there was much space for the new people to come up and take over.

But genetic scientists also say that everybody is by nature capable of living at least three hundred years—and remain young. Old age can be abolished. And it will be a great revolution, because if an Albert Einstein can go on working for three hundred years, if a Gautam Buddha can go on preaching for three hundred years, if all the great poets and mystics and scientists and painters can go on working, refining their methods, refining their language, their poetry, refining their techniques, technology, the world will be immensely rich.

This is a very great wastage as it is now. When a man really comes of age, death starts knocking on his door. It is very strange—it brings new people who know nothing. Now bring them up, educate them, train them, discipline them, and by the time they are really mature, retire them. When they are really capable of doing something, the time of retirement comes. And after retirement nobody lives more than ten or fifteen years, because after retirement one becomes absolutely useless, and he himself starts feeling a burden on the children, on the society. He loses all his respectability, prestige, power. He becomes an outsider, an unwelcome guest who is just reluctant to die.

You may not be aware that the generation gap has never been in existence in the past. The generation gap is a new phenomenon that has come into existence just now because people are living longer. Now a ninety-year-old father...three other generations have come into existence. His son is seventy years old, his grandson is fifty years old, his great grandson is thirty years old. Now the distance is so great that the great grandson has no connection at all: Who is this old man, and why does he go on hanging around?—an unnecessary trouble and always irritated, always angry, always ready to freak out. What purpose is there?

In the past, people never saw four or five generations together; hence there were no generation gaps. I don't even know the name of my great grandfather. I asked my father. He said, "I don't know myself. The names that you know are the names I know. More than that, I know nothing."

Now in the Caucasus, where there are a few people who are living at the age of one hundred and eighty, what do you think? Seventh, eighth generation children will be in their houses and they will not recognize them. These people should have been in their graves long before—that was the usual way. So foreigners are living in the house, one house. They don't speak each other's language because the times have changed. They don't understand each other's fashions, they don't understand each other's music, each other's religion. There is nothing in common at all.

If we continue to live accidentally, then the situation is going to become worse. It is better that society takes a new formulation, a totally new program. Old programs have failed. The commune is the new unit of the world. No more family, no more nation—communes and an international humanity.

The commune is decisive in creating what is needed, because right now you need doctors but doctors are not there. Engineers are unemployed because there are too many engineers; or you need engineers and engineers are not there. There is no planning of life, it is just going zigzag, accidentally. That's why there are so many unemployed people; otherwise there is no need, there should not be a single person unemployed. You should not produce more people than you can give employment to.

As machines are becoming more and more capable of doing the work of man, more efficient than man, without asking for higher wages, without going on strike, without changing shifts—twenty-four hours they go on producing; a single machine can work in place of a thousand people—more and more people will be becoming unemployed.

It is better to plan, so that you have only as many people as you need. And why not have the best? Why not drop this mob that surrounds the earth? This mob is the most dangerous thing, because it plays into the hands of any cunning politician.

The mob has no mind of its own, no intelligence of its own. We can create individuals with great intelligence, individuality, and each generation will be a better generation than the outgoing one. Then evolution will be in leaps and bounds; otherwise we are stuck. We have been stuck for thousands of years, only things go on growing—better cars, better airplanes, better bombs, but not better human beings.

If man is stuck and everything goes on growing, it is a dangerous situation. Man will be burdened with his own progress, with his own technology, with his own science. Man should also grow; man should always remain ahead.

I understand Devageet's concern, but I don't agree with it. I always see a ray of light in the darkest night. And howsoever dark the night may be, there is always a possibility for the dawn to be very close.

I am in favor of every scientific progress, but the progress should be in the hands of creative people, the progress should not be in the hands of war-mongers. War can now be stopped and war-mongers can disappear. This is possible for the first time in the history of man. Hence, don't be afraid of totalitarian people.

It is true that genetic scientists cannot say anything definitely; perhaps in the future they will be more definite. It is a very new discovery, to read the future possibilities in human sperm. It is just the beginning. Perhaps within five years, ten years' time, what we are now just able to say as a possibility we will be able to say as a certainty. Then the nurture is in our hands, so that we can give a harmonious nurture, knowing the possibility, and create more harmonious beings.

Devageet, look positively at things, don't look negatively.

I have heard....

Hymie Goldberg goes to visit his gay friend lying on his deathbed. Hymie's friend is whining and snivelling about the negative side of his life. Hymie, in an attempt to cheer up his friend, says in a consoling voice, "Don't just look at the dark side of things. At least your AIDS test was positive!"

Just look at the positive side, whatever the circumstance may be.

The genetic scientists have also been trying to change the program which is already determined by biology. Up to now they have not been able to split the living cell of the sperm, just the way they have been able to split the atom. But it took three hundred years of physical research to split matter into atomic energy. It may take a few years, but I am absolutely certain that they will be able to split the living human sperm also. And once they are able to split it, they can reprogram it. The whole program is there.

You will be surprised to know that once in a while there are twins born. Twins are of two types: two-egg twins and one-egg twins. Once in a while this accident happens, that the mother releases two eggs—which is very rare. Then naturally two male sperm enter the two eggs. These are also twins, but they have differences because their mother cells are different. Once in a while just one egg is released but two male sperm reach the mother cell exactly at the same time, so as the door opens they get in. Then a rare variety of twins is born, which is one-egg twins.

They look exactly similar, and experiments on these twins have given great insights to genetic scientists, because these twins... One may be living in Europe and one may be living in China. In China there may be some disease that the child falls sick of. In Europe the disease is not there, but the twin child in Europe will fall sick of the same disease of which his brother has fallen sick—without being informed about it.

They will have at the same time colds, headaches, and they will die almost simultaneously, wherever they are. That gave genetic scientists the first idea that there must be a fixed and determined program; otherwise how is it happening? It cannot be infection because one boy is in Europe and one boy is in China. Why should they have headaches at the same time? They feel angry at the same time, they feel sad at the same time.

It seems it is beyond their capacity to be sad or angry—it is something in their program. They die almost simultaneously; at the most the difference has been found to be three months, but not more than that. Mostly it is the same day, but at the most the difference has been only of three months.

If we can change the genetic program, life can have a very different flavor. We can change the many stupidities that man is prone to. We can change man's lust for power, we can change man's desire to be somebody special, we can change jealousy— we can simply remove it and we can put in new qualities, as a program.

It is not that you are not ashamed of your jealousy, your anger, your lust for power, but what can you do? Somehow you feel that you are caught in some blind force that drives you nuts.

A husband and wife were having a fight. "Look, honey," the husband said, "can't we discuss this sensibly?"

"No, no, no!" she shouted, and stamped her foot. "Every time we discuss things sensibly I lose."

We have to change the woman's genetic program, so that every time she discusses sensibly she does not have to lose. She knows perfectly well, that "sensibly" is not the way to win. Behave as crazily as possible, do absolutely absurd things. Make the whole neighborhood know and the husband will be afraid, and he will say, "You are right."

They know the whole question is not being sensible or not sensible. The question is, who wins. Victory decides whether your means were right or wrong. But this has to be changed. This destroys something in the individuality of women. Reason will give them a beauty. Intelligence will give them something that will make them not only physically beautiful, but will make them also mentally more developed.

Otherwise, even the most beautiful women in the world are not capable of having a good conversation. They are mostly vegetables. They look beautiful, so it is always good to look at somebody else's woman because you are only looking; the other man knows how she behaves, what she says, what she does. But she is not responsible, it is the biological programming.

Genetics relieves you of your burden. Man has a very chauvinistic, egoistic idea about himself. That is his program. It makes him look very stupid.

Jerry was visiting his married friends Ethel and Richard. "Rich, I can't help it," said Jerry, "but Ethel really turns me on. If I could pinch her on the backside just once, I would give her five thousand dollars."

"For that kind of money," said Richard, "I don't think Ethel would mind. Go ahead, pinch her."

Ethel leaned over a chair, lifted her skirt and exposed her bare behind. Jerry took a long, thoughtful look at it. Finally, after about five minutes he said, "I just can't do it."

"Why not?" asked Richard. "Have you not got the nerve? "

"It is not that," said Jerry. "I have not got the money."

But the desire is there...what to do?

I am in every way in favor of genetic reprogramming of men and women. What kind of nonsense is this? Pinching! And in every crowd men are doing that. Every woman knows when she has been pinched, and she cannot conceive what this man is getting out of it. But the man is ready to give five thousand dollars, which he has not got! Some blind force which is not within his control...

Unless we change the whole program of men and women, we will not have a new world. We have to drop all fears. And I repeat again, never act out of fear. Any action out of fear is going to lead us backwards.

Act with consciousness, cautiously. Use every preventive measure so that what you are doing cannot be misused, but don't look backward. Life is ahead and in the future. Because of this point I have angered all of India's Gandhians; if it weren't for this they would be my followers. Even the president of the ruling party and the ministers and the chief ministers, all used to attend the meditation camps.

But the day I started saying things against Mahatma Gandhi, they became afraid. Nobody answered me, but they became afraid: "You should not say anything against Mahatma Gandhi."

I said, "I am not saying anything against him, but what he is proposing is a backward step, taking man back to primitive ages, making him more barbarous. He is already barbarous."

But the people who are acting out of fear think perhaps it is good that all scientific progress is stopped and all scientific technology is drowned in the ocean, and man goes back to when there was not even kerosene oil, when there were no clothes—you had to spin your own clothes.

If you spin your own clothes eight hours per day, in a year you will be able to clothe yourself, your bed, but what you are going to eat? And if some day you fall sick, from where will you get the medicine? And what are you going to feed to your children, and how are you going to feed your old father and mother and your wife? And how are the children going to be educated?—who is going to pay their fees and their expenses? One man has to be involved for eight hours just making his own clothes.

Such a society will be so poor...no education. But Gandhi is against education because education is being misused. His whole philosophy is based on fear: anything that can be misused... But you are talking such nonsense—anything can be misused. There is not a single thing in the world which cannot be misused. If you are just living in paranoia then everything has to be renounced.

In my home town, my father's shop was in front of a row of barber's saloons. And I used to go to those saloons because they used to have newspapers, magazines for their customers. I was not a customer of anybody, but I used to go for their magazines and their newspapers.

The principal of my school used to come to a certain shop for his beard to be shaved, his hair to be cut. But he never talked with the barber. And that barber was so talkative that a thing that could be done in five minutes would take fifty minutes, because he would go so slow and he would talk so much. And I saw that my principal was simply saying, "Yes, yes, mmm, yes..." He would never talk to him.

One day I caught hold of him outside the shop. I said, "This is strange, he goes on saying anything and you don't even talk."

He said, "You don't understand, that man is almost mad. You have not heard what he is saying. He is saying anything—I have not asked, I am not interested. And moreover, he has that big razor blade just near my throat. If I say something... And he looks like a very angry man, because he is always saying that 'We will destroy this whole government,' and this and that, so I have to simply be silent.

"Politics cannot be discussed, religion cannot be discussed, because he is such a fanatic. Instead of cutting my hair he will cut my throat! He will not take a single moment to think. My life is at risk and you are asking me, 'Why don't you talk to that man?'"

I said, "Then I can help you to find a better barber." He said, "No, I don't want to change either because this one I am accustomed to. I don't know about others." He was an outsider in the city.

So he said, "I don't want to get into trouble. This one at least simply talks and bores me, takes a long time—but no harm... And I have become accustomed."

I said, "It is up to you; otherwise I have an acquaintance with a barber. If you want he can do you without taking any money."

He said, "I don't want to take any risk. A man who can do it without money—he is dangerous from the very beginning. Why should he do it without taking money?"

I said, "Because he does things. He is an opium addict."

What punks are sometimes doing in the West now, that man in that village was doing fifty years ago. He would simply cut off half of your hair—just on any whim. And when you asked, "What are you doing?" when you looked in the mirror, "What have you done?" he would say, "Don't be angry. If you don't like it, don't give me any money, I have done it for free. You get lost. I have wasted my time and you don't have any appreciation."

But, the man could not move in that situation because punks were not known at that time. They are not known even now in India. Sometimes he would cut half the mustache and would say,

"Wait, I am coming." And the man would say, "Where are you going?"

He said, "I am just going to take a cup of tea. Just sit down. And I have cut half the mustache considerably, so that you cannot escape from here."

I have seen people sitting for hours. Once he was gone, he was gone. If he came back on the same day it was great fortune, because he was such a good conversationalist that anybody could catch hold of him and he would sit there and he would start talking. And he would forget all about his shop. I have seen people sitting there for hours, and they would say, "My God, is this man going to come back or not?"

I said, "Don't be worried, he will come because he has to close the shop."

They said, "To close the shop? That is the whole day. Shops are closed at eight o'clock in the evening and now it is just ten o'clock in the morning."

I said, "You can go and have your lunch and come back. You don't be worried, he will come."

And mostly it happened that he would come only when the shop had to be closed; otherwise that was an illegal act, keeping the shop open after eight o'clock. That's why he had to come. And he would see the man sitting there and say, "What are you doing, when there is nobody here? Who are you? What are you doing here?"

The man said, "Have you forgotten me? In the morning you cut half of my mustache." He would say, "Yes, I remember. I remember that sometime I cut half of somebody's mustache. So you are that fellow! Come tomorrow, because now it is time to close the shop. Otherwise I will be in trouble—the police may come and you will be in trouble. Why are you sitting here?"

The man said, "This is strange." So he said, "You can go, I will not charge you." And the man had wasted the whole day!

He said, "At least cut my half mustache. And I had not told you to cut my mustache at all. I had come to have my beard shaved. I have been always proud of my mustache and you have destroyed my mustache."

The barber was a very philosophical man. He said, "Don't be worried, hairs grow. They will grow again. Don't be worried, I have not cut off your nose. Just feel fortunate, because once the nose is cut off, it never grows." He would cut half of the mustache and the man would rush out angry—but what to do? And the principal knew about it, he had heard many stories.

When I told him that "This is the place," he said, "You are getting me into trouble. Can't you stop making trouble for people? You create trouble for your teachers, you create trouble for your fellow students. I don't get in your way. Every day I receive reports against you. I just go on keeping them in the file, because I don't want to encounter you unnecessarily. I have not done any harm to you and you are introducing me to that opium addict."

There are all kinds of people in the world. These people could have been totally different, just they need a different program from the very beginning.

There are so many criminals in your jails. In America, they have so many jails and so many criminals that American judges have been telling the government, "If you don't create more jails, close the courts, we cannot send anybody to jail—there is no space. Once we send somebody to jail, we have to release somebody else, although he should still remain in jail for two or three years. We have to release him just to make space for the new criminal."

The whole world is full of jails, and these people only have the wrong genetic program. They are victims of a blind biological force. And, Devageet, do you want to continue this accidental humanity? Don't you want it to be well-planned—intelligently, consciously? I understand your fear, but that can be avoided. That should be avoided. But progress cannot be dropped.

In every way we can create a man who is really a superman, who has never existed except in the dreams of great poets and great mystics. That superman has to be made a reality. Genetic science and engineering can help immensely.

Little Eddy was doing his arithmetic homework. "Three plus one, the son of a bitch, is four," he was saying. "Three plus two, the son of a bitch, is five. Three plus three, the son of a bitch, is six." And so on.

Eddy's mom was horrified when she overheard him. The next day she went to see what kind of arithmetic his teacher was teaching.

"I don't quite understand where Eddy has picked this language up," said the teacher. "I simply teach the children to say: three plus one, the sum of which is four; three plus two, the sum of which is five."

But not only little Eddy, even your oldest citizens of the world are living in such a misunderstanding about everything.

In spite of the dangers we have to take steps to change this situation. Man's intelligence is absolutely dependent on his genetic heritage. We can have as many Albert Einsteins as we need, we can have as many Rabindranath Tagores as we need, we can have as many Nijinskys as we need. The world can be such a beautiful place. But certainly there are risks and there are dangers, and I am aware of them more than you are aware of them, Devageet. But still, I want to take all the risks because man has nothing to lose—he has got nothing. So why be so much afraid? He has everything to gain and he has nothing to lose.

The risk can be taken—yes, with consciousness, with awareness. Hence I am teaching all the time how to be more aware, how to be more conscious, because much has to be done once we have a certain portion of humanity alert and conscious. Those will be our guardians, our guards against technology being used in any way for evil purposes.

We can take every protective measure, but we cannot go backwards.

Okay Maneesha?

Yes, Osho.

11

COMPASSION—LOVE COME OF AGE

The gesture of giving is of tremendous importance once you know that giving does not take anything from you; on the contrary, it multiplies your experiences. But the man who has never been compassionate does not know the secret of giving, does not know the secret of sharing.

Beloved Osho,

Buddha was saying again and again to his disciples that meditation and compassion should grow side by side. These days I have been feeling Your compassion as never before, and I have also been feeling the urge to start learning from it, at least the ABC. For now, the only thing that makes me feel close to it are those warm tears that flow down my cheeks as I look at You.

Beloved, can You please talk about compassion, and how to go into it from the stage I'm at.

Chidananda, Gautam Buddha's emphasis on compassion was a very new phenomenon as far as the mystics of old were concerned. Gautam Buddha makes a historical dividing line from the past; before him meditation was enough, nobody had emphasized compassion together with meditation. And the reason was that meditation brings enlightenment, your blossoming, your ultimate expression of being. What more do you need? As far as the individual is concerned, meditation is enough. Gautam

Buddha's greatness consists in introducing compassion even before you start meditating. You should be more loving, more kind, more compassionate.

There is a hidden science behind it. Before a man becomes enlightened, if he has a heart full of compassion there is a possibility that after meditation he will help others to achieve the same beautitude, to the same height, to the same celebration as he has achieved. Gautam Buddha makes it possible for enlightenment to be infectious. But if the person feels that he has come back home, why bother about anybody else?

Buddha makes enlightenment for the first time unselfish; he makes it a social responsibility. It is a great change. But compassion should be learned before enlightenment happens. If it is not learned before, then after enlightenment there is nothing to learn. When one becomes so ecstatic in himself then even compassion seems to be preventing his own joy—a kind of disturbance in his ecstasy... That's why there have been hundreds of enlightened people, but very few masters.

To be enlightened does not mean necessarily that you will become a master. Becoming a master means you have tremendous compassion, and you feel ashamed to go alone into those beautiful spaces that enlightenment makes available. You want to help the people who are blind, in darkness, groping their way. It becomes a joy to help them, it is not a disturbance.

In fact, it becomes a richer ecstasy when you see so many people flowering around you; you are not a solitary tree who has blossomed in a forest where no other tree is blossoming. When the whole forest blossoms with you, the joy becomes a thousandfold; you have used your enlightenment to bring a revolution in the world. Gautam Buddha is not only enlightened, but an enlightened revolutionary.

His concern with the world, with people, is immense. He was teaching his disciples that when you meditate and you feel silence, serenity, a deep joy bubbling inside your being, don't hold onto it; give it to the whole world. And don't be worried, because the more you give it, the more you will become capable of getting it.

The gesture of giving is of tremendous importance once you know that giving does not take anything from you; on the contrary, it multiplies your experiences. But the man who has never been compassionate does not know the secret of giving, does not know the secret of sharing.

It happened that one of his disciples, a layman—he was not a sannyasin, but he was very much devoted to Gautam Buddha—said, "I will do it...but I want just to make one exception. I will give all my joy and all my meditation and all my inner treasures to the whole world—except my neighbor, because that fellow is really nasty."

Neighbors are always enemies. Gautam Buddha said to him, "You forget the world, you simply give to your neighbor."

He said, "What are you saying?"

Buddha said, "If you can give to your neighbor, only then will you be freed from this antagonistic attitude towards a human being."

Compassion basically means accepting people's frailties, their weaknesses, not expecting them to behave like gods. That is cruelty, because they will not be able to behave like gods and then they will fall in your estimation, and they will also fall in their own self-respect. You have dangerously crippled them, you have damaged their dignity. One of the fundamentals of compassion is to make everybody dignified, everybody aware that what has happened to you can happen to him; that he is not a hopeless case, that he is not unworthy, that enlightenment is not to be deserved, it is your very self-nature.

But these words should come from the enlightened man, only then can they create trust. If they come from unenlightened scholars, they cannot create trust. The word, through the enlightened man, starts breathing, starts having a heartbeat of its own. It becomes living, it goes directly into your heart—it is not an intellectual gymnastics. But with the scholar it is a different thing. He himself is not certain of what he is talking about, what he is writing about. He is in the same uncertainty as you are.

Gautam Buddha is one of the landmarks in the evolution of consciousness; his contribution is great, immeasurable. And in his contribution, the idea of compassion is the most essential. But you have to remember that by being compassionate you don't become higher; otherwise you spoil the whole thing. It becomes an ego trip. Remember not to humiliate the other person by being compassionate; otherwise you are not being compassionate, behind the words you are enjoying their humiliation.

Compassion has to be understood, because it is love come of age. Ordinary love is very childish, it is a good game for teenagers. The faster you grow out of it the better, because your love is a blind biological force. It has nothing to do with your spiritual growth; that's why all love affairs turn in a strange way, become very bitter.

That which was so alluring, so exciting, so challenging, for which you could have died...now you could still die—but not for it, you could die to get rid of it.

A great psychologist, Alfred Adler, went to a madhouse to see in what condition the mad people were, what their problems were, and if he and his understanding about man's psychology could be of any help.

The superintendent knew he was a world famous figure...but there happened to be a very strange case. He saw a man behind bars, in a cell, who was keeping a photograph on his chest—and tears were coming from his eyes. Alfred Adler knew the man, because the man was a professor in the university where Alfred Adler had addressed the professors many times. He was a very learned man. What had happened to this poor guy?

The superintendent said, "It is a very complicated and strange story. When you know the whole of it, you will not be able to believe it. He loved a woman—the picture is of that woman. He still loves her, he cannot forget her for a moment. He never loses hold of the picture; even in the night he sleeps with the picture. And these tears...one cannot believe how many tears he has. They seem to be inexhaustible, they go on flowing. Because the woman refused to marry him, that triggered something in him and he went mad.

"Now he does not talk to anyone. We have tried in every possible way to break the ice and somehow bring him back to normality, but he does not talk, he does not want to see anybody. If you go in front of him, he closes his eyes. He wants to see only his beloved. That picture is more real to him than anything else in the world. And that 'no' is hurting him so deeply...he eats well but he goes on losing weight. He has become almost a skeleton."

Alfred Adler said, "I knew the man before; he was a perfectly healthy, a robust person. He has aged as if he had skipped at least twenty years. He was young when I knew him, just a year ago."

The superintendent said, "He is simply committing slow suicide. That 'no' has been too heavy; he really loved the woman."

They moved on, and in the second cell there was a man rolling around like a maniac, hitting the walls, beating the bars, shouting as loudly as he could, "Just leave me! I want to do one thing only—to kill that woman!"

And the superintendent said to Alfred Adler, "You will be surprised now, really surprised. The woman who refused the first man—and he has gone mad because he could not conceive of his life without her—is the same woman this man married. And just within six months of marriage things have gone so poisonous that he wants to murder her. He has made efforts to murder her; he was caught by the police and forced into the madhouse."

Alfred Adler, in his autobiography, remembers the incident, and he said, "What kind of love is this? They both loved, but the first one, to whom she said no, still loves her; and the second one, to whom she said yes, wants to kill the woman. That is his only goal in life. He said, 'Any day, someday you will let me out. My only project is to kill that woman and surrender myself to the police. You can shoot me, you can hang me, whatever you want to do—I am no longer interested. But let me do at least one thing first—kill that woman. She destroyed my peace, my life, my joy, everything.'"

Love is a blind force. The only successful lovers have been those who never succeeded in getting their beloveds. All the great stories of lovers: Lailla and Majnu, Shiri and Farhad, Soni and Mahival...these are the three Eastern stories of great love. But all the three never could get together; society, parents, everything became a barrier. And I think perhaps it was good. Once lovers get married, then there is no love story left.

Majnu was fortunate that he never got hold of Lailla. What happens when two blind forces come together? Because both are blind and unconscious, the outcome cannot be a great harmony. The outcome can only be a battlefield of domination, of humiliation, of all kinds of conflicts.

The very word 'compassion' will remind you about passion. When passion becomes alert and aware, the whole energy of love comes to a refinement; it becomes compassion.

Love is always addressed to one person, and its deepest desire is to possess that person. But the same is the case from the other side—and that becomes the cause of creating a hell.

Compassion is not addressed to anybody. It is not a relationship, it is simply your very being. You enjoy being compassionate to the trees, to the birds, to the animals, to human beings, to everybody—unconditionally, not asking for anything in return. Compassion is a freedom from blind biology. Before you become enlightened, you should keep alert that your love energy is not repressed. That's what old religions have been doing: they teach you condemnation of your love. So you repress your love energy, and that is the energy which can be transformed into compassion. But by condemnation there is no possibility of transformation.

So your saints are absolutely without any compassion; in their eyes you will not see any compassion. They are absolutely dry bones, with no juice at all. To live with a saint for twenty-four hours is enough to experience what hell is like. Perhaps people are aware of this fact, so they immediately touch the feet of the saint and run away.

One of the great philosophers of our age, Bertrand Russell, has emphatically declared, "If there is hell and heaven, I want to go to hell." Why? Just to avoid the saints, because heaven will be full of all these dead, dull, dusty, saints. And Bertrand Russell thinks, "I could not tolerate this company even for a minute. And to think of eternity, forever, to be surrounded by these corpses, who don't know any love, who don't know any friendship, who never go on holidays..."

A saint always remains seven days a week a saint. It is not allowed for him that at least on one day, Sunday, he should enjoy being a human being. No, he remains stiff, and this stiffness goes on growing as time passes.

Bertrand Russell's choice to be in hell I appreciate very much, because I can understand what he means by it. He is saying that in hell you will find all the juicy people of the world—the poets, the painters, the rebellious spirits, the scientists, the creative people, the dancers, the actors, the singers, the musicians. Hell must be really a heaven, because heaven is nothing but a hell!

Things have gone so wrong, and the basic reason for their going wrong is that love energy has been repressed. Gautam Buddha's contribution is, "Don't repress your love energy. Refine it, and use meditation to refine it."

So side by side, as meditation grows it goes on refining your love energy and makes it compassion. Before your meditation reaches to its highest climax and explodes into a beautiful experience of enlightenment, compassion will be very close. It will become possible for the enlightened person to let his energies flow—and now he has all the energies of the world—through the roots of compassion, to anyone who is ready to receive. Only this type of man becomes a master.

To become enlightened is simple, but to become a master is a very complex phenomenon, because it needs meditation plus compassion. Just meditation is easy, just compassion is easy; but both together, simultaneously growing, becomes a complex affair.

But the people who become enlightened and never share their experience because they don't feel any compassion, don't help the evolution of consciousness on the earth; they don't raise the level of humanity. Only the masters have been able to raise consciousness. Whatsoever small consciousness you have, the whole credit goes to the few masters who managed to remain compassionate, even after their enlightenment. It will be difficult for you to understand, because enlightenment is so absorbing that one tends to forget the whole world.

One is so utterly satisfied that he does not have any space to think of all those millions who are also groping for the same experience—knowingly, unknowingly. Rightly or wrongly, but a compassion remains present; then it is impossible to forget those people. In fact, this is the moment when you have something to give, something to share. And sharing is such a joy. You have known through compassion, slowly slowly, that the more you share, the more you have. If you can share your enlightenment too, your enlightenment will have much more richness, much more aliveness, much more celebration, many more dimensions.

Enlightenment can be one-dimensional—that's what has happened to many people. It satisfies them, and they disappear into the universal source. But enlightenment can be multidimensional, it can bring so many flowers to the world. And you owe something to the world because you are sons of this earth.

I am reminded of Zarathustra's saying, "Never betray the earth. Even in your highest glory, don't forget the earth; it is your mother. And don't forget the people. They may have been hindrances, they may have been enemies to you; they may have tried in every way to destroy you; they may have already crucified you, stoned you to death, or poisoned you—but don't forget them. Whatever they have done, they have done in an unconscious state. And if you cannot forgive them, who is going to forgive them? And your forgiving them is going to enrich you immeasurably."

Chidananda, you are asking, "Gautam Buddha was saying again and again to his disciples that meditation and compassion should grow side by side." That's his uniqueness amongst all other mystics.

"These days I have been feeling your compassion as never before, and I have also been feeling the urge to start learning from it, at least the ABC. For now, the only thing that makes me feel close to it are those warm tears that flow down my cheeks as I look at you. Beloved, can you please talk about compassion, and how to grow into it from the stage I am at?"

You simply allow it to grow on its own. You are in a right space; those tears are indications. If you start doing something to make the process of growth faster, you may damage the whole thing. It is almost like a gardener—he cannot pull up his plants to make them grow faster. The pulling may destroy the whole plant. It may come out of the earth with the roots, and you may not be able to give it life again. The gardener has to take care; he has to water, he has to give nourishment, he has to give all kinds of manure, but he has not to touch the plant. The plant will grow on its own, it is a spontaneous growth.

You are feeling that the seed has broken, and perhaps just two green leaves have sprouted out of the earth. Rejoice, and in every way support it, but don't try to hurry up the process. There are processes which cannot be hurried—you can kill them. They are so delicate that they grow only on their own. You can support them, you can put around them everything that they need, but leave them absolutely to themselves.

You are exactly in a right space. Enjoy your tears, enjoy your laughter—and not only when you are with me. Slowly, slowly bring the same space with other people. Perhaps they will not be able to understand you. They may start consoling you, "Chidananda, don't cry. What has happened? Has your girlfriend left you? Or are you in some financial trouble?" Just tell them that your girlfriend has not left, that you are not in financial trouble, but thank them for their sympathy. Tell them your tears are not of sadness or failure; your tears are out of your joy.

Joy is the nourishment for your compassion...a very subtle food. Sing, dance, play on musical instruments, and all this will support the delicate phenomenon that has already been born in you. But don't do anything to hurry up the process, because that hurrying up comes from the mind. The mind is always in a hurry, the mind is always speeding; but all great things grow very slowly, very silently, without making any noise.

Just watch that anything that goes against compassion you don't give any support to. Jealousy, competition, an effort to dominate—all that goes against compassion. And you will know immediately because your compassion will start wavering. The moment you feel your compassion is shaky, you must be doing something that is going against it. You can poison your compassion by stupid things, which don't give you anything except anxiety, anguish, struggle, and a sheer wastage of a tremendously precious life.

A beautiful story for you:

Paddy came home an hour earlier than usual and found his wife stark naked on the bed. When he asked why, she explained, "I am protesting because I don't have any nice clothes to wear."

Paddy pulled open the closet door. "That's ridiculous," he said, "look in here. There is a yellow dress, a red dress, a print dress, a pantsuit...Hi, Bill!" And he goes on, "A green dress..."

This is compassion!

It is compassion to his wife, it is compassion to Bill. No jealousy, no fight, just simply, "Hi, Bill! How are you?" and he goes on. He never even enquires, "What are you doing in my closet?"

Compassion is very understanding. It is the finest understanding that is possible to man.

As he was approaching an intersection, the man's car lost its brakes and bumped into the rear of a car with "Just Married" written all over it. The damage was slight but the man sincerely offered his apologies to the newlywed couple.

"Aw, it doesn't matter," replied the husband. "It has been one of those days."

An understanding, a deep understanding that now everything is possible... Once one is married, then he can expect all kinds of accidents. The greatest accident has already happened—now nothing matters.

A man of compassion should not be disturbed by small things in life, which are happening every moment. Only then, in an indirect way, are you helping your compassionate energies to accumulate, to crystallize, to become stronger, and to go on rising with your meditation.

So the day the blissful moment comes, when you are full of light, there will be at least one companion: compassion. And immediately a new style of life...because now you have so much that you can bless the whole world.

Although Gautam Buddha insisted consistently, finally he had to make a division, a categorization amongst his disciples. One category he calls *arhatas*; they are enlightened people, but without compassion. They have put their whole energy into meditation, but they have not listened about compassion. And the other he calls *bodhisattvas*; they have listened to his message of compassion. They are enlightened with compassion, so they are not in a hurry to go to the other shore; they want to linger on this shore, with all kinds of difficulties, to help people. Their boat has arrived, and perhaps the captain is saying, "Don't waste time, the call has come from the other shore, which you have been seeking all your life."

But they persuade the captain to wait a little, so that they can share their joy, their wisdom, their light, their love with all those people who are also searching the same. This will become a trust in them: "Yes, there is another shore, and when you are ripe a boat comes to take you to the other shore. There is a shore of immortals, there is a shore where no misery exists, there is a shore where life is simply a moment-to-moment song and a dance. Let me at least give them a little taste before I leave the world."

And masters have tried in every possible way to cling to something so that they are not swept away to the other shore. According to Buddha, compassion is the best, because compassion is also a desire, in the final analysis. The idea to help somebody is also a desire, and while you can keep the desire you cannot be taken to the other shore. It is a very thin thread that keeps you attached to the world. Everything is broken, all chains are broken—a thin thread of love... But Buddha's emphasis is, keep that thin thread as long as possible; as many people that can be helped, help them.

Your enlightenment should not have a selfish motive, it should not be just yours; you should make it shared as widely, to as many people as possible. That's the only way to raise the consciousness on the earth—which has given you life, which has given you the chance to become enlightened.

This is the moment to pay back something, although you cannot pay back everything that life has given to you. But something—just two flowers, in gratitude.

Beloved Osho,

Being here with You, I find myself more and more often in moments of let-go. It seems that in these moments my mind loses all its power, and I can watch overwhelming waves of energy vibrating within my body. I suddenly become aware of the earth beneath my feet, and it feels as if I am connected with existence itself, as if I am one with existence.

Beloved Master, would You please talk to us again about the state of let-go and melting into existence.

L okita, the question that you have asked is, "Being here with you, I find myself more and more often in moments of let-go." That's the very purpose of this place, that's the very purpose of me lingering on this shore. My boat has long been waiting. So if you are feeling moments of let-go, that is a good beginning, in the right direction.

"It seems that in these moments my mind loses all its power, and I can watch overwhelming waves of energy vibrating within my body." It happens, when you are in a let-go, that the mind has no power over you. The mind becomes impotent, it loses all its power. And the same power is felt vibrating all over your body. So these are exactly the right symptoms.

"I suddenly become aware of the earth beneath my feet, and it feels as if I am connected with existence itself, as if I am one with existence." Just, please drop those words, "as if." When you feel that you are one with existence, what is the need of "as if"? That destroys the very beauty of the experience.

Perhaps you are afraid to say with certainty that "I feel one with existence," but here you have to be exactly authentic and sincere in whatever you say. It is also possible in the beginning that when such experiences happen, you yourself are uncertain whether you are imagining, hallucinating, because you have never felt one with existence before. So just to avoid showing your confusion, uncertainty, you can use "as if." But "as if" is a very poor expression.

There is a great book of philosophy called *As If*. And the whole book is filled with great statements, but all their greatness is destroyed because the man goes on saying "as if": As if there is a God... It is better to say "There is no God," or "There is a God." But "as if there is a God" keeps God in a limbo, hanging in the middle. Neither do you give him reality, nor do you take him as unreal. You make him a hypothesis.

So I would like you, when these experiences happen to you again—and they will be happening—to drop the idea of "as if." Feel the experience in its totality, and attain to some certainty. That certainty will make the experience happen more often. And as it happens more often, more certainty...and a point comes such that even if the whole world denies it, it does not matter. Your certainty is far bigger, far more crystallized than the whole world. It is not a question of voting, you know it. I want you to be aware of the dangers of "as if." That will never allow you a certain ground to stand on; you will be always wavering, wishy-washy.

You are asking me to talk about "the state of let-go and melting into existence." There is no need to talk about it, it is almost happening to you. It is better to let it happen. No talk can be a substitute for actual experience. But mind plays all kinds of games before it leaves you, it tries in every possible way to keep you entangled. That "as if" is coming from the mind.

The experience of becoming one with existence is coming from a different source—beyond mind. You drop that "as if" and listen to the source beyond, and allow these moments more and more to take possession of you, without any fear.

That is one of the greatest advantages of being with a master. Alone, you will become so afraid—perhaps you are going insane, how can you be one with existence? And if you talk to people, say that you are being one with existence, they will say, "Shut up. Don't say it to anybody, otherwise you will be sent to a psychiatric hospital. One with existence?"

It is too big even if you say, "I am feeling one with this tree." They will say, "My God! Lokita has gone out of her mind. Something has to be done to put her back into her normal senses. How can you be one with a tree, or a mountain, or the ocean?"

But in this place...this is a communion, a gathering of fellow seekers, where everybody's experience is going to help everybody else to experience the same things without any fear. I am here to tell you whether you are moving in the right space or not, and I say with an absolute guarantee, you are moving in a right space.

Those moments are beautiful when you feel the let-go. These are the things you cannot do. Let-go is not something that you can manage to do—that will not be let-go; you are still the manager. It is something like sleep: either it comes or it does not come. You cannot force it to come, you cannot threaten it to come, you cannot blackmail it to come; you have just to wait silently, trustingly. Whenever it comes, it comes. It is beyond your powers of doing.

And let-go is a far greater relaxation than sleep. These moments are happening to you without any effort, that is their beauty. If you don't listen to your mind and its doubts, those moments will become bigger and bigger. Finally, one starts feeling oneself in a let-go twenty-four hours a day.

Don't ask me to talk about the state of let-go, because that may give you clues, and you may start forcing them to happen more often—because the beauty of those moments is not of this world. The nourishment that comes in those moments is divine.

So there is no need, because they are happening on their own. Just beware, when you become in those moments, a nobody. A let-go means the ego has disappeared. You will feel oneness with existence, because the ego is the only barrier. Once the ego disappears, you are one with the earth, you are one with stars, you are one with everything all around.

One Zen master, Bokoju, was very puzzling to his students, his disciples. He had a big monastery and a great name as an enlightened master—and he was. Every morning, when he would open his eyes, the first thing he would say was, "Bokoju, are you still here?"

"Yes, sir." He would answer it too.

The disciples said, "This is madness."

Finally they gathered courage and asked, "Everything is okay that you say, but what you do every day in the morning is absolutely inconceivable to us, it looks insane. You are Bokoju and you ask, 'Bokoju, are you still here?' And you yourself say, 'Yes, sir.'"

Bokoju laughed. He said, "I become so relaxed and so one with existence that a question arises in me: is Bokoju still in the same old personality? So just to hear my own voice, I ask, 'Bokoju, are you still here?' And when I hear the question I say, 'He is here.' That's why I say, 'Yes, sir.'"

"You need not think that I am insane. In the day I am so much engaged with your problems, from the morning until late in the night. But in the night I am left alone, in a let-go. In the morning I have to remind myself, 'Who am I? And what am I doing here? Who is this fellow who is waking up?' So I have made it a strategy. I forget everything, but I keep on remembering only one thing: the name of Bokoju. The day I forget that name also, you can prepare for a funeral."

They were very much shocked. They said, "No, we don't want you to forget. You continue as many times as you want to ask; it is your business, in your room."

He said, "Not many times, just one time."

And the last day, on the day he died, he did not ask. He woke up, and the disciples waited: "What happened to his lifelong habit? 'Bokoju, are you still here?' And he himself answers, because there is nobody else, 'Yes, sir.' What has happened? He has not asked it." They gathered courage again, and one disciple asked, "You have forgotten something."

He said, "I have not forgotten, but Bokoju is no more here. And no one is here to answer 'Yes, sir.'

"I have only been waiting for the morning so that I can see you for the last time and bless you for the last time; otherwise in the middle of the night I was evaporating. Now it is not a meaningful question to ask. So come close to me, receive my blessings; Bokoju is going, and from tomorrow this room will be empty to the ordinary eyes—but to those who had loved me, it will be still full of my presence. And those who have loved me totally, they may even hear every morning a sound coming from nowhere, 'Bokoju are you still here?'—'Yes, sir.'"

And the story is that only two disciples were able to hear it after he was dead, disposed of, but many felt his presence. Those two disciples became enlightened very soon.

Even when you are becoming one with existence, it does not mean you lose your individual being. You lose only your periphery, your center remains always there. But in such a harmonious state with existence, you can say that you have become one with it.

So this is a very vulnerable state for you. Perhaps this anecdote may help you:

"I have to take every precaution to avoid pregnancy," confided a woman to her friend.

"But hasn't your husband just had a vasectomy?" asked her friend.

"Yes," replied the woman, "and that's why I have to take every precaution."

You have to take every precaution not to get entangled with doubts, questions, and the mind. And just enjoy the feeling of let-go. The more you enjoy it, the more it will be coming to you.

The mind is the only problem in the growth of your spiritual being. The mind is continuously lying. Even when there is something real happening, it becomes very much afraid, it creates all kinds of doubts, because its life is at risk.

Two women in a restaurant were having an intense conversation. One said to the other, "Why don't you go to him in a perfectly straightforward way and lie about the whole thing."

Great advice! But that's what the mind goes on doing to everybody.

Hymie Goldberg thought he had the perfect marriage, until he moved from New York to California and discovered he still had the same milkman.

Don't trust the mind—a perfect marriage! And everything else is just a lie. Mind is a lying energy. Respect with certainty the experiences that are happening to you—the let-go, and because of the let-go the feeling as if the separation has disappeared.

That "as if" is not your feeling; that "as if" is an insertion by your mind. You are feeling with absolute certainty that the separation has disappeared and you are one with existence. So all that you have to do is to drop your "as if," and to not allow your mind to interfere and disturb a beautiful phenomenon that is going to grow in you.

Okay, Maneesha?

Yes, Osho.

AN INVITATION TO EXPERIENCE

OSHO Never Born Never Died
Only Visited This Planet Earth Between Dec 11, 1931 - Jan 19, 1990

Osho is an enlightened Mystic.

During the course of thirty years of talks to seekers and friends, Osho would answer their questions, or comment on the teachings of the world's great sages and scriptures. His talks continue to bring fresh insight to everything, from the obscure Upanishads to the familiar sayings of Gurdjieff, from Ashtavakra to Zarathustra. Osho speaks with equal authority on the Hassids and the Sufis, the Bauls, Yoga, Tantra, Tao and Gautama the Buddha. And ultimately, Osho concentrates on transmitting the unique wisdom of Zen, because, He says, Zen is the one spiritual tradition whose approach to the inner life of human beings has weathered the test of time and is still relevant to contemporary humanity. Zen is another word for the original Hindi word Dhyana. In English you may translate it as 'meditation', but Osho says this is a poor translation. So call it Dhyana or Zen or whatever you may wish - Osho's emphasis is on *experiencing*.

Osho settled in Pune in 1974, and disciples and friends from all over the world gathered around Him to hear His talks and practice His meditation techniques for the modern man. Western therapeutic group processes, classes and trainings were gradually introduced so bridging the wisdom and understanding of the East with the scientific approach of the West. And now Osho Commune International has evolved into the world's largest centre for meditation and spiritual growth, and offers hundreds of different methods for exploring and experiencing the inner world.

Every year, thousands of seekers from all over the world come to celebrate and meditate together in Osho's buddhafield. The commune grounds are full of lush green gardens, pools and waterfalls, elegant snow-white swans and colourful peacocks, as well as beautiful buildings and pyramids. Such a peaceful and harmonious atmosphere makes it very easy to experience the inner silence in a joyful way.

For detailed information to participate in this Buddhafield contact:

OSHO COMMUNE INTERNATIONAL
17 Koregaon Park, Pune-411001, MS, India
Tel: 020 6128562 Fax: 020 6124181
E-mail: visitor@osho.net Website: www.osho.com

BOOKS BY OSHO

English Language Editions

EARLY DISCOURSES AND WRITINGS
A Cup of Tea
Dimensions Beyond The Known
From Sex to Superconsciousness
The Great Challenge
Hidden Mysteries
I Am The Gate
The Inner Journey
The Long and the Short and the All
Psychology of the Esoteric
Seeds of Wisdom

MEDITATION
The Voice of Silence
And Now and Here (Vol 1 & 2)
In Search of the Miraculous (Vol 1&.2)
Meditation: The Art of Ecstasy
Meditation: The First and Last Freedom
The Path of Meditation
The Perfect Way
Yaa-Hoo! The Mystic Rose

BUDDHA AND BUDDHIST MASTERS
The Book of Wisdom
(combined edition of Vol 1 & 2)
The Dhammapada (Vol 1-12)
   The Way of the Buddha
The Diamond Sutra
The Discipline of Transcendence (Vol 1-4)
The Heart Sutra

BAUL MYSTICS
The Beloved (Vol 1 & 2)

KABIR
The Divine Melody
Ecstasy: The Forgotten Language
The Fish in the Sea is Not Thirsty
The Great Secret
The Guest
The Path of Love
The Revolution

JESUS AND CHRISTIAN MYSTICS
Come Follow to You (Vol 1-4)
I Say Unto You (Vol 1 & 2)
The Mustard Seed
Theologia Mystica

JEWISH MYSTICS
The Art of Dying
The True Sage

WESTERN MYSTICS
Guida Spirituale On the Desiderata
The Hidden Harmony
   The Fragments of Heraclitus
The Messiah (Vol 1 & 2) Commentaries on
   Khalil Gibran's The Prophet
The New Alchemy: To Turn You On
   Commentaries on Mabel Collins'
   Light on the Path
Philosophia Perennis (Vol 1 & 2)
   The Golden Verses of Pythagoras
Zarathustra: A God That Can Dance
Zarathustra: The Laughing Prophet
   Commentaries on Nietzsche's
   Thus Spake Zarathustra

SUFISM
Just Like That
Journey to the Heart (same as Until You Die)
The Perfect Master (Vol 1 & 2)
The Secret
Sufis: The People of the Path (Vol 1 & 2)
Unio Mystica (Vol 1 & 2)
The Wisdom of the Sands (Vol 1 & 2)

TANTRA
Tantra: The Supreme Understanding
The Tantra Experience
   The Royal Song of Saraha
   (same as Tantra Vision, Vol 1)
The Tantric Transformation
   The Royal Song of Saraha
   (same as Tantra Vision, Vol 2)
The Book of Secrets: Vigyan Bhairav Tantra

THE UPANISHADS
Behind a Thousand Names *Nirvana Upanishad*
Heartbeat of the Absolute *Ishavasya Upanishad*
I Am That *Isa Upanishad*
The Message Beyond Words: A Dialogue with
   the Lord of Death
Philosophia Ultima *Mandukya Upanishad*
The Supreme Doctrine *Kenopanishad*
Finger Pointing to the Moon
   Adhyatma Upanishad

That Art Thou *Sarvasar Upanishad, Kaivalya
    Upanishad, Adhyatma Upanishad*
The Ultimate Alchemy
    Atma Pooja Upanishad (Vol 1 & 2)
Vedanta: Seven Steps to Samadhi
    Akshaya Upanishad

TAO

The Empty Boat
The Secret of Secrets
Tao: The Golden Gate (Vol 1 & 2)
Tao: The Pathless Path (Vol 1 & 2)
Tao: The Three Treasures (Vol 1- 4)
When the Shoe Fits

YOGA

The Path of Yoga (previously Yoga: The Alpha
    and the Omega Vol 1)
Yoga: The Alpha and the Omega (Vol 2-10)

ZEN AND ZEN MASTERS

Ah, This!
Ancient Music in the Pines
And the Flowers Showered
A Bird on the Wing (same as Roots and Wings)
Bodhidharma: The Greatest Zen Master
Communism and Zen Fire, Zen Wind
Dang Dang Doko Dang
The First Principle
God is Dead: Now Zen is the Only Living Truth
The Grass Grows By Itself
The Great Zen Master Ta Hui
Hsin Hsin Ming: The Book of Nothing
    Discourses on the Faith-Mind of Sosan
I Celebrate Myself: God is No Where,
    Life is Now Here
Kyozan: A True Man of Zen
Nirvana: The Last Nightmare
No Mind: The Flowers of Eternity
No Water, No Moon
One Seed Makes the Whole Earth Green
Returning to the Source
The Search: Talks on the 10 Bulls of Zen
A Sudden Clash of Thunder
The Sun Rises in the Evening
Take it Easy (Vol 1) Poems of *Ikkyu*
Take it Easy (Vol 2) Poems of *Ikkyu*
This Very Body the Buddha *Hakuin's Song
    of Meditation*
Walking in Zen, Sitting in Zen
The White Lotus
Yakusan: Straight to the Point of Enlightenment
Zen Manifesto: Freedom From Oneself
Zen: The Mystery and the Poetry of the Beyond
Zen: The Path of Paradox (Vol 1, 2 & 3)
Zen: The Special Transmission

ZEN BOXED SETS

The World of Zen (5 volumes)
Live Zen
This. This. A Thousand Times This
Zen: The Diamond Thunderbolt
Zen: The Quantum Leap from Mind to No-Mind
Zen: The Solitary Bird, Cuckoo of the Forest
Zen: All The Colors Of The Rainbow (5 vol.)
The Buddha: The Emptiness of the Heart
The Language of Existence
The Miracle
The Original Man
Turning In
Osho: On the Ancient Masters of Zen (7 vol.)
Dogen: The Zen Master
Hyakujo: The Everest of Zen - With Basho's
    haikus
Isan: No Footprints in the Blue Sky
Joshu: The Lion's Roar
Ma Tzu: The Empty Mirror
Nansen: The Point Of Departure
Rinzai: Master of the Irrational
Each volume is also available individually.

RESPONSES TO QUESTIONS

Be Still and Know
Come, Come, Yet Again Come
The Goose is Out
The Great Pilgrimage: From Here to Here
The Invitation
My Way: The Way of the White Clouds
Nowhere to Go But In
The Razor's Edge
Walk Without Feet, Fly Without Wings
    and Think Without Mind
The Wild Geese and the Water
Zen: Zest, Zip, Zap and Zing

TALKS IN AMERICA

From Bondage To Freedom
From Darkness to Light
From Death To Deathlessness
From the False to the Truth
From Unconsciousness to Consciousness
The Rajneesh Bible (Vol 2-4)

THE WORLD TOUR

Beyond Enlightenment *Talks in Bombay*
Beyond Psychology *Talks in Uruguay*
Light on the Path *Talks in the Himalayas*
The Path of the Mystic *Talks in Uruguay*
Sermons in Stones *Talks in Bombay*
Socrates Poisoned Again After 25 Centuries
    Talks in Greece
The Sword and the Lotus *Talks in the Himalayas*
The Transmission of the Lamp *Talks in Uruguay*

OSHO'S VISION FOR THE WORLD
The Golden Future
The Hidden Splendor
The New Dawn
The Rebel
The Rebellious Spirit

THE MANTRA SERIES
Hari Om Tat Sat
Om Mani Padme Hum
Om Shantih Shantih Shantih
Sat-Chit-Anand
Satyam-Shivam-Sundram

PERSONAL GLIMPSES
Books I Have Loved
Glimpses of a Golden Childhood
Notes of a Madman

INTERVIEWS WITH THE WORLD PRESS
The Last Testament (Vol 1)

**INTIMATE TALKS BETWEEN MASTER
AND DISCIPLE - DARSHAN DIARIES**
A Rose is a Rose is a Rose
Be Realistic: Plan for a Miracle
Believing the Impossible Before Breakfast
Beloved of My Heart
Blessed are the Ignorant
Dance Your Way to God
Don't Just Do Something, Sit There
Far Beyond the Stars
For Madmen Only
The Further Shore
Get Out of Your Own Way
God's Got A Thing about You
God is Not for Sale
The Great Nothing
Hallelujah!
Let Go!
The 99 Names of Nothingness
No Book, No Buddha, No Teaching, No Disciple
Nothing to Lose but Your Head
Only Losers Can Win in This Game
Open Door
Open Secret
The Shadow of the Whip
The Sound of One Hand Clapping

The Sun Behind the Sun Behind the Sun
The Tongue-Tip Taste of Tao
This Is It
Turn On, Tune In and Drop the Lot
What Is, Is, What Ain't, Ain't
Won't You Join The Dance?

COMPILATIONS
After Middle Age: A Limitless Sky
At the Feet of the Master
Bhagwan Shree Rajneesh: On Basic Human
  Rights
Jesus Crucified Again, This Time in Ronald
  Reagan's America
Priests and Politicians: The Mafia of the Soul
Take it Really Seriously

GIFT BOOKS OF OSHO QUOTATIONS
A Must for Contemplation Before Sleep
A Must for Morning Contemplation
India My Love

PHOTOBOOKS
Shree Rajneesh: A Man of Many Climates,
  Seasons and Rainbows *through the eye of
  the camera*
Impressions... *Osho Commune International
  Photobook*

BOOKS ABOUT OSHO
Bhagwan: The Buddha for the Future
  by Juliet Forman
Bhagwan Shree Rajneesh: The Most
  Dangerous Man Since Jesus Christ
  by Sue Appleton
Bhagwan: The Most Godless Yet the Most
  Godly Man *by Dr. George Meredith*
Bhagwan: One Man Against the Whole Ugly
  Past of Humanity *by Juliet Forman*
Bhagwan: Twelve Days That Shook the World
  by Juliet Forman
Was Bhagwan Shree Rajneesh Poisoned by
  Ronald Reagan's America?
  by Sue Appleton
Diamond Days With Osho
  by Ma Prem Shunyo

GIFTS
Zorba the Buddha Cookbook

For Osho's books and audio/video tapes contact:
SADHANA FOUNDATION
17 Koregaon Park, Pune-411001 MS, India
Tel: 020 6128562, Fax: 020 6124181
E-mail: distrib@osho.net Website: www.osho.com